Plan & Go | High Sierra Trail

All you need to know to complete the Sierra Nevada's best kept secret

Zebulon Wallace

sandiburg press

Plan & Go | High Sierra Trail

All you need to know to complete the Sierra Nevada's best kept secret

Copyright © 2016 by Zebulon Wallace and sandiburg press

ISBN 978-1-943126-02-6

Front and back cover photos copyright © 2016 by Zebulon Wallace
Unless otherwise stated, all interior photos by Zebulon Wallace

Editor: Kevin Muschter

Published by sandiburg press
www.sandiburgpress.com

Cover photos: Kern River Valley (front); Hamilton Gorge (back)

SAFETY NOTICE: This book describes physically challenging activities in remote outdoor environments which carry an inherent risk of personal injury or death. While the author(s) and sandiburg press have made every effort to ensure that the information contained herein was accurate at the time of publication, they are not liable for any damage, injury, loss, or inconvenience arising directly or indirectly from using this book. Your safety and health during preparations and on the trail are your responsibility. This book does not imply that any of the trails described herein are appropriate for you. Make sure you fully understand the risks, know your own limitations, and always check trail conditions as they can change quickly.

Content

Welcome

This book is a structured guide to hiking the High Sierra Trail (HST), a stunning 72-mile path through the wilderness of the Sierra Nevada mountain range in California. Written to inspire and enable novice and experienced hikers alike, the book provides a clear depiction of the trail's unique features and conditions along with comprehensive step-by-step instructions to help ensure you will not only complete the HST, but also have an amazing time throughout your journey.

The following chapters will empower you with the information and tools needed to get you from where you sit reading this book to the starting trailhead at Crescent Meadow, packed and prepared for your unforgettable time on the HST. From logistical considerations, such as permits, starting and ending points, trail sections, and campsites, to practical advice regarding training, food and water resupply, and appropriate gear, this book provides essential details to assist hikers with planning their own High Sierra adventure. You won't find this to be a comprehensive historical or topographical guide, but you will get a sound understanding of the skills and equipment needed to undertake a hike of this magnitude.

The High Sierra Trail has all the memory-making potential of a much longer hike, packaged into a job-friendly, one-week vacation. There is perhaps no better way to laterally cross the immense Sierra Nevada range on foot. The journey begins amidst giant redwoods in Sequoia National Park and ends at Mt. Whitney, the highest peak in the contiguous United States at 14,505 feet (4,421m). You will wake up to sunrise on your tent flaps, fall asleep to the breeze rustling the lodgepole pines, stand on mountain tops with the world stretched out before you, become hypnotized by the sounds of your own footsteps on the crushed granite path, go in and out of day dreams while your mind and the trail wander through the wilderness, and come home with some great stories that won't quickly be forgotten.

Upper Hamilton Lake

1. Introduction

Sequoia National Park in California is the second oldest National Park in the United States and the home of the HST. The trail's 72 miles take you all the way from the park's western edge amidst the awe-inspiring giant sequoias to its eastern edge, soaring 14,505 feet into the sky atop Mt. Whitney. As you pass through Kaweah Gap on day two or three of your journey, keep an eye out to your left for a small bronze plaque mounted in plain sight on the side of a large boulder. The plaque commemorates Colonel George Stewart – the man who is widely considered the father of Sequoia National Park.

Colonel Stewart, who lived just 35 miles from the park in the town of Visalia, California, successfully argued that the giant sequoias were worthy of preservation both for their natural beauty and for the important role they played in managing melting snowpack that would otherwise damage local agriculture. It was Colonel Stewart's efforts that drove legislation through Congress which would eventually create Sequoia National Park.

It wasn't until the park's expansion some twenty five years after its founding in 1890 that the High Sierra Trail would come into existence. It would be among the first trails to be hewn from the land at great cost and effort, principally for the recreational enjoyment of the people. In 1927, the then Superintendent of Sequoia National Park, Colonel John R. White, announced the creation of a "High Sierra Trail" – a trail that would enable visitors to traverse Sequoia National Park from one end to the other.

Work on the HST was ultimately completed in the summer of 1932. Although, as a consequence of the Great Depression and subsequent financial troubles facing the nation, the original path for the trail envisioned by Colonel White was never realized. Instead, the existing system of trails beyond Kaweah Gap was simply improved upon. The result is the rather circuitous route the trail follows to join the Kern River south of the Kaweah Peaks, rather than a more direct route which would have connected Kaweah Gap to Junction Meadow.

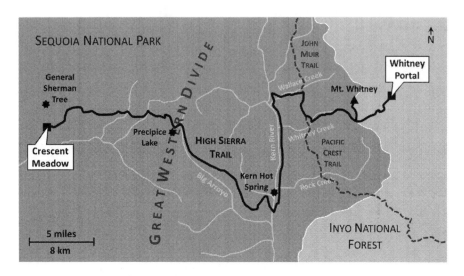

Figure 1 – Overview Map of the High Sierra Trail

My journey towards hiking the HST began 35 years ago at a campground near Rock Creek Lakes Resort in the Sierra Nevada, about 30 miles north of Bishop, California. I was less than one year old. I have gone back to this same campground every year since. Despite these annual trips to the Sierra, I had really only seen the same small sliver of it again and again – the area around Rock Creek. It was like I had been visiting the same theme park for over thirty years and only going on the rides I had been on before. I was ready to try a different ride – one that excited and intimidated me at the same time.

In January of 2014, the memories of my 2012 adventures were beginning to be become too hard to recall and my adventureless 2013 was beyond repair. It was time to refresh myself with a new outdoors' experience, I just had to figure out where I was going. Since losing my job in Corporate America wasn't on my bucket list, I decided that it would be better to find a trail that could work with the reality of my nine-to-five professional career. The trick was that I needed to cram all that excitement and adventure into a week's worth of vacation days. Enter the High Sierra Trail.

Before feeling up to the challenge of the HST, I spent a few months researching and planning to ensure that I not only finished the trail, but also had a great time along the way. Preparation was key. This book will give you the knowledge that I accumulated before and after my trip on the HST, as well as some additional tips, recommendations, and information that will get you ready for the hike of a lifetime.

For the purposes of this book, we will only cover the trail as hiked from west to east, beginning at Crescent Meadow and ending at Whitney Portal. This is the direction most people choose for the simple purpose that it is much easier to get a wilderness permit for Crescent Meadow than for Whitney Portal. Permits for Whitney Portal are always in high demand since it is the most direct way to summit Mt. Whitney.

Following this introduction, Chapter 2 describes the physical challenges of the trail and gives guidance on estimating the time it will take to complete it. Chapter 3 lets you know what to expect regarding weather and trail conditions, campsites, and water. Your initial estimate of trail hiking days allows you to prepare the Long Lead Items of Chapter 4, such as permits and travel plans. How to prepare for all this physically and logistically is the topic of Chapter 5. Then, Chapter 6 takes a close look at gear options for the High Sierra. Finally, Chapter 7 offers some personal experiences and anecdotes from my own 5-day HST adventure.

To me, step one in any great adventure is deciding to go, step two is some basic planning, and step three is going. You bought this book and you're reading it, you're now in step two of your HST adventure if you weren't already. You're over half way there. Keep going and don't forget to email me a picture of yourself at the top of Mt. Whitney.

-Zeb

Visit *www.PlanAndGoHiking.com* for more information and pictures.

2. Summary of the Challenge

The High Sierra Trail is a 72.2-mile (116.2 km) trail that connects the Western and Eastern Sierra Nevada[1] in California. The trail is hiked from west to east, beginning at Crescent Meadow in Sequoia National Park and ending at Whitney Portal at the base of Mt. Whitney in the Inyo National Forest. The vast majority of the trail travels west to east with the notable exception of the Kern River Valley section, which takes you north along the Kern River to where you will intersect the John Muir Trail, a 210-mile trail from Yosemite Valley to Mt. Whitney.[2]

a. Requirements

You will probably be traveling between ten and twelve hours per day. Unless you're taking a break or are asleep, you're walking. Assuming you cover around ten miles per day, you'll be walking around 20,000 steps per day for seven days – 140,000 steps total. This is the equivalent of roughly two and half marathons. Hikes of this duration and distance will challenge your body in a way that shorter hikes simply can't. Anything that normally hurts when you hike will have plenty of time to hurt on the HST. Be prepared to deal with ailments that can range from the typical blisters, bruises, and aches to more severe injuries, like sprained joints.

Hiking the HST also requires the ability to deal with altitude. You'll have several days where you ascend and descend thousands of feet and will reach elevations as high as 14,505 ft. (4,421m) at the summit of Mt. Whitney. If you are afraid of heights, I would recommend that you be honest with yourself about this before you go on the trail. If you don't know whether you are, the trail is going to give you a couple of chances to find out.

---

[1] The Sierra Nevada is a large mountain range that extends approx. 400 miles from Tehachapi, CA, on the southern end to Fredonyer Pass on the northern end.
[2] Please see *Plan & Go: The John Muir Trail* for additional information on this amazing trail.

In addition, you should expect and be prepared to deal with the following:

- Severe temperature swings, from low 20s at night to 90+ degrees Fahrenheit during the day (-6 to 32+ degrees Celsius)
- Carrying a 35-45lbs backpack during a strenuous, multi-hour hike for multiple days in a row.
- Setting up a tent in the middle of the forest, without a designated tent-spot already prepared for you.
- Using a portable gas stove to cook all meals.
- Purifying your own water, which you will collect from streams and lakes.
- Carrying and eating freeze-dried/lightweight food while enduring repeated and intense physical activity.
- Not "showering" for multiple days in a row and using the woods as your toilet.

Assuming you are hiking the HST during the late Spring to early Fall season (like most everyone does), you shouldn't need any special gear beyond what you would normally take on a multi-night backpacking trip in the High Sierra. Specific gear recommendations will be covered in detail in Chapter 6. The HST is a Class 1/Class 2 trail according to the Yosemite Decimal System (YDS), which means no sections of the trail will require you to have any climbing gear or experience[3].

> ❗ Due particularly to the duration and distance from civilization, I do not recommend making the HST your first multi-day backpacking experience. Consider doing at least one overnight trip before the HST so that you have a general sense of what it takes to live in the wild for a couple of days.

---

[3] The YDS is a system used for rating the difficulty of trails with 1 being the easiest (hiking on a well-maintained trail) and 5 being the hardest (vertically climbing that requires ropes and other technical equipment).

b. Time

The standard time that people allot to complete the HST is six to seven days, although five-day and eight or more day trips are certainly possible. A six-day trip works out to an average of a little more than eleven miles of hiking per day, which, when combined with the pack weight and elevation gain and loss, requires you to be a strong hiker. At this pace, you should have enough time to reach your camp each night while still having a little extra time to relax during the day. This pace will probably not allow you to take side trips or follow a very leisurely schedule. If the latter is what you're looking for, you'll probably want to budget seven or more days for your hike.

Estimating your days on the trail is the first step in planning your own HST adventure. Figure 2 is intended to provide guidance for an initial assessment. Selecting your age and corresponding fitness level will give you an idea of approximately how long it will take you to complete the trail. For example, a 40-year-old person of average fitness can expect to spend roughly seven days on the trail.

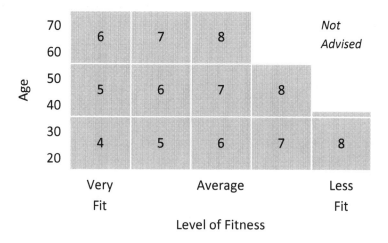

Figure 2 – Estimate of Trail Days on the HST

Once you have determined your estimate of trail days (ETD), you can calculate your average daily mileage by dividing the total distance of the HST by your ETD:

Average miles per day = 72 miles / ETD

Continuing the above example leads to an average of 72/7 = 10.3 miles per day. While this is a good initial estimate, additional factors need to be taken into consideration as they will impact how far you will go each day and, consequently, the duration of your hike. Here are a few examples:

- Number and duration of stops you plan to make (e.g., for taking photos, appreciating the scenery, relaxing)
- Difficulty of a particular trail section (i.e., elevation gain/loss)
- Whether you plan to take any side trips or rest days

I took five days to do the HST, hiking solo with no side trips or long stopovers. Given the total distance and elevation change, this is probably on the more aggressive end of how quickly people complete this trail. In talking to people on the trail and doing research for this book, it seems that most people complete the HST in six to seven days. Side trips or an especially leisurely pace could easily push that up to eight days or more.

c. Budget

When planning a trip on the HST, you need to consider how much money you'll need and want to spend. Your biggest expenses will probably be traveling to and from the trail, lodging before and after the hike, buying gear that you don't currently own and/or upgrading to lighter gear.

Travel costs will vary significantly depending on where you are traveling from and are likely to be a fairly inflexible portion of your total budget. Gas for your car costs what it costs, as does public transportation such as busses, shuttles, and trains. Depending on your pre and post trip plans, you may need to consider whether you will get a hotel room or camp before you set off on the trail and after you finish. Both options have different budgetary implications.

You will not have much flexibility with regards to when you hike the HST. Late June and all of July and August is pretty much the window you want to shoot for to minimize the chances that you'll encounter impassible snow at the higher elevations. This time period also happens to be when most people hit the road for summer travel. Try booking flights and hotels early and consider camping before and after your trip to do what you can to control these costs.

Gear, unlike travel, presents you with a lot of opportunities to save money or spend a small fortune. Your gear budget will depend primarily on two factors: a) How much money you want to spend, and b) How lightweight you want your gear to be. With hiking gear, cost and weight are inversely related. Generally speaking, the lower the weight, the higher the cost. The closer you get to "ultralight" equipment (a designation we will use here to mean the most lightweight equipment that you can purchase), the more exponentially expensive the gear becomes. This trend will be most obvious with tents, sleeping bags, backpacks, and jackets.

If you don't already own a full kit of lightweight backpacking gear, you generally have three options: borrow, rent, or buy. If you're hiking on a budget, consider asking friends if they have some lightweight gear you can borrow or visit your local backpacker supply store to see if you can rent some top tier gear for a fraction of what it would cost you to purchase. Ideally, you would want to take the absolutely lightest set of gear possible that still meets your personal requirements (warmth, comfort, fit, etc.) and the requirements of the trail (weather, terrain, etc.).

Table 1 below provides an overview of the general pricing ranges for major pieces of gear. The differences between low cost and high cost in the table have more to do with weight than it does with the quality. Generally speaking, the higher the price, the lighter the gear. More detailed information and gear recommendations can be found in Chapter 6.

Gear Item	Low Cost	High Cost	Best Value[4]
Backpack	$150	$350	$200-$300
Tent	$150	$450	$250-$300
Sleeping Bag	$100	$400	$200-$300
Sleeping Pad	$20	$150	$40-$75
Hiking Shoes	$75	$200	$100-$150
Hiking Poles	$50	$200	$100-$150
Jacket (warm)	$100	$400	$150-$200
Jacket (shell)	$100	$400	$150-$200
Hiking shirt	$20	$80	$40-$60
Hiking pants	$50	$100	$75-$100
Water Filter	$25	$100	$50-$100
Bear Canister	$75	$350	$75-$100
Stove	$40	$150	$40-$100
Pot/Kitchen	$25	$100	$50-$75
Water Bladder	$25	$50	$35
Headlamp	$25	$150	$50-$100
Total	**$1,030**	**$3,630**	**$1,605-$2,345**

Table 1 – Gear Cost Ranges: Low, High, and Best Value

By comparison, buying the necessary *food supplies* for your trip will represent a relatively small portion of the budget. Freeze-dried meals are very convenient but certainly more expensive (approx. $7-10 per meal) than home-made meals. If dehydrating your own food is not an option, there are cheap backpacking meal alternatives you can opt for instead (e.g., macaroni and cheese, top ramen). Section 5b *Food* will discuss a variety of options and sample meal plans.

---

[4] "Best Value" is purely based on my own personal determination of a good balance between quality, weight, and price. It is generally closer to the top of the line than the bottom, but it's by no means the absolute top of the line.

3. What to Expect

This chapter describes the highlights and unique characteristics of the HST. You will get a clear picture of what to look forward to and what to look out for when attempting to hike this trail. The information provided will also assist you in choosing appropriate gear and setting realistic goals.

a. Trails & Navigation

Although relatively less traveled than some of the more popular Sierra Nevada trails (like the John Muir Trail), the HST is well-worn, making it both easy to follow and easy to travel on. It is a Class 1/Class 2 trail according to the Yosemite Decimal System, which means no climbing is required, and your hands will not be needed except occasionally for balance.

Trail Length

Online or in other publications you may find references to the HST being only 70 miles long, not 72.2 miles as I have indicated in this book. My reference to the 72.2-mile distance comes directly from the National Park Service website[5] and measures the trail from the trailhead at Crescent Meadow in Sequoia National Park to the trailhead at Whitney Portal.

Other resources may indicate that the trail ends about 49 miles after Crescent Meadow where it intersects the John Muir Trail around Wallace Creek. Like two rivers merging together, it could be argued that at this juncture you actually move onto the John Muir Trail for the rest of your trip. However, since this intersection is still deep in the wilderness, it's not really possible to end your journey there. As a result, when people refer to the HST, they typically include the section of the John Muir Trail that runs from the intersection to Whitney Portal. For the purposes of this book, the High Sierra Trail will follow this common convention.

---

[5] See Appendix G *Links & References* for detailed website information.

Trail Access/Exit

The official starting point of the HST is the trailhead at Crescent Meadow in Sequoia National Park. You may come across some references to starting the HST in Wolverton or Panther Meadow in Sequoia National Park. While you can join the HST from these alternative starting points by using the myriad of trails that connect up near the beginning of the HST, Crescent Meadow is the only official starting point of the trail. The official ending point of the HST is the trailhead at Whitney Portal, located at the base of Mt. Whitney.

Crescent Meadow	Whitney Portal
Located in Sequoia National Park at 36.55288° N 118.748° W, about 55 miles northeast of Visalia, CA.	Located in the Inyo National Forest at 36.5892° N 118.2258° W, about 11.5 miles due west of Lone Pine, CA.

Table 2 – Starting and Ending Trailheads

[!] Once you pass Mehrten Creek, about 6.5 miles (10.5km) from the starting trailhead, you will not have another exit point until you reach Whitney Portal. If you run into trouble on the HST and need help, there are ranger stations at *Bearpaw Meadow* and *Crabtree Meadow*.

Trail Conditions

The HST will challenge your feet and test your stability with a variety of path materials over its 72-mile course. While the vast majority of the trail is well-compacted dirt, at different times, you could be walking on sand, mud, crushed rock, wet stepping stones at river crossings, bridges, snow, leaf litter, gravel, and boulders. The path is well-maintained and built to last, so you won't be in a constant state of scrambling to maintain your footing as you teeter on the edge of chasms. You will, however, want to keep a close eye on the ground in front of you as you simultaneously try to take in your magnificent surroundings and try to avoid tripping over things in the middle of the trail. Those roots come out of nowhere!

The route is well-graded and utilizes switchbacks liberally to help you make the numerous ascents and descents that you will encounter during your trip. While this means that you will generally be able to enjoy a mildly sloping incline or decline, it doesn't mean that you'll be treated to a city-sidewalk experience. Even the most minor incline can feel comically difficult when you're hauling a heavy backpack through oxygen deficient air at over 12,000 ft. (3,650m). There are several points on the HST where you will experience big elevation gains or  losses within a single day *and* over a relatively short distance. To help you plan for these physically taxing events, below is an elevation profile of the trail along with a list of some of the most significant elevation gains and losses you will encounter.

Highest/Lowest Points:

- Mt. Whitney: 14,505 ft. (4,421m)
- Upper Funston Meadow: 6,650 ft. (2,027m)

Biggest Elevation Gains:

- Hamilton Lakes to Kaweah Gap: 2,464 ft. (751m)
- Junction Meadow to Guitar Lake: 3,422 ft. (1,043m)
- Guitar Lake to Mt. Whitney Summit: 3,009 ft. (917m)

Biggest Elevation Losses:

- Moraine Lake to Upper Funston Meadow: 2,654 ft. (809m)
- Mt. Whitney Summit to Whitney Portal: 6,132 ft. (1,869m)

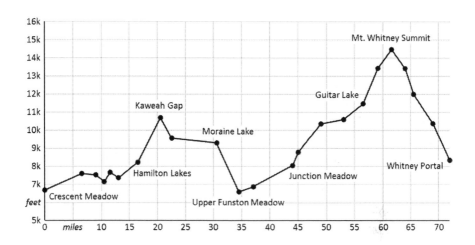

Figure 3 – HST Elevation Profile

While a smattering of trees will flank many sections of the HST, relatively few sections will have any consistent, dense shade. The most heavily shaded portions of the trip will be from Crescent Meadow to Hamilton Lakes and from Upper Funston Meadow to Junction Meadow. Shade will be available at many other times along the HST, but you may have to seek it out and take advantage of it when you find it.

Shade will generally be available at the lower elevations where trees are still abundant and large. As you ascend to higher elevations, you will be passing above treeline (~12,000 ft./3,650m), the elevation at which trees no longer grow in this part of the Sierra Nevada. Around that elevation, the most you can hope for is the occasional stunted-growth tree that will look more like a knee-high bush. Once you get a ways above the treeline, you won't even find these smaller trees.

The lack of trees also means that you will probably experience the most wind exposure at higher elevations. The summit of Mt. Whitney can be particularly windy, which, when combined with the lower temperatures at higher elevation, can make it extremely cold even on a clear, sunny day.

Navigation

There are a number of points along the HST where it will intersect with other trails and give you the opportunity to accidentally make a wrong turn. Unfortunately, the few signs that you will see along the route are not always clear and can be confusing. As a rule of thumb, whenever you encounter a fork in the trail, pull out your map and use it to verify which direction you should be heading. Appendix D provides an overview of all the trail crossings to look out for, listed in the order in which you will encounter them. Unless specifically indicated otherwise, don't take any of those trail crossings as they will lead you off the HST.

> [!] While the descriptions above will be helpful in giving you a basic understanding of the HST, this information is not meant to replace the maps that you need to take with you on the trail. See the maps entry in Section 6f *Other Essentials* for details and recommendations.

Trail Use Restrictions

When on the HST, there are some rules you must follow. These rules help protect the wilderness and minimize the impact of year after year of visitors so that everyone can enjoy the wilderness in as close to its natural state as possible.

- To prevent erosion and preserve vegetation, do not short cut trails.
- Do not build rock cairns or other trail markers
- Pack out all trash, including toilet paper
- Wheeled and motorized vehicles are prohibited
- Pets are not allowed
- Possession of firearms and other weapons is prohibited
- Possession of bear spray is prohibited

b. Points of Interest

There are a number of highlights along the trail that may invite hikers to incorporate additional time in their itineraries for further exploration.

The Largest Trees in the World

At 26 stories tall, as wide as a city street, and between 1,800 and 2,700 years old, the largest of the giant sequoia are an absolute must-see before you set out on the HST. The General Sherman Tree in Sequoia National Park is the largest tree in the world (by volume), according to the National Park Service website. After you pick up your permit and are on the way to the trailhead, take a quick stop to see this immense tree. It is well worth the short detour before you hit the trail.

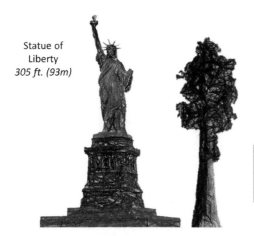

Statue of Liberty
305 ft. (93m)

General Sherman Tree
275 ft. (84m)

Height above base	274.9 ft.	83.8m
Circumf. at ground	102.6 ft.	31.3m
Max. diam. at base	36.5 ft.	11.1m
Estim. trunk volume	52,508 cu. ft.	1,487m³

Figure 4 – General Sherman Tree Comparison and Dimensions

Precipice Lake

Approximately 19 miles from Crescent Meadows, Precipice Lake is an early milestone on the trail that's worth writing home about. Renowned photographer Ansel Adams brought this stunning and little-visited lake to the world's attention in his famous work *Frozen Lake and Cliffs*, which showcases the lake against its sheer, granite-wall backdrop.

Kern Hot Spring

Always wanted to skinny dip in a hot spring but never found a secluded enough place? Try the Kern Hot Spring – 30 miles on foot from the nearest town. Although this amazing little gem is just off of the trail near mile 37, the lovingly-built little wooden privacy fence and the fact that I saw exactly zero other human beings the entire day led me to believe that I was probably safe from ending up on the internet.

Mt. Whitney

The 14,505-foot (4,421m) Mt. Whitney is the highest summit in the contiguous United States – a trophy that hikers from inside and outside the country are eager to bag each year. Unlike most of them, you'll be summiting the mountain from the backside, avoiding the infamous permit-clamoring madness of the Whitney Portal route. From the summit, you'll be treated to an incredible, 360-degree panoramic view of the Sierra Nevada. While there, take a moment to explore the Smithsonian Institution Shelter, a stone hut built in the early 1900s to house scientific studies of high-altitude phenomena as well as spectroscopic observations of Mars. Just think of how much fun you'll have telling lesser mortals about the shack on the mountain top that you've seen with your own eyes.

c. Weather

The best time to hike the HST is between late June and early September. During these months, you will have a very low chance of encountering any significant snow. The weather will be warmer and the days will be longer, giving you more time to hike and reducing the amount of gear you have to carry for cold and/or snowy conditions.

Temperature

The elevation change you will experience on the HST means that you're in for some pretty wild swings in temperature. You should be ready to deal with hiking in hot temperatures and going to sleep in the freezing cold. Crescent Meadow and the Kern Valley can get up into the 70-90s °F (20-

30s °C), while Kaweah Gap, Trail Crest, and the summit of Mt. Whitney could give you plenty of teeth chattering potential with temps down into the 20s °F (-7 °C) or lower.

Table 3 below shows average annual temperatures for the Lodgepole Campground in Sequoia National Park (6,700 ft./2,042m). In order to estimate the temperatures along the trail, it is helpful to use a lapse rate. As a rule of thumb, deduct 5°F for every 1,000 ft. in elevation gain (3°C for every 300m) from the respective temperature of your hiking month.

Month	°F (high/low)	°C (high/low)
January	39 / 16	4 / -9
February	41 / 17	5 / -8
March	45 / 22	7 / -6
April	50 / 26	10 / -3
May	59 / 33	15 / 1
June	68 / 39	20 / 4
July	76 / 45	24 / 7
August	76 / 44	24 / 7
September	69 / 38	21 / 3
October	58 / 31	14 / -1
November	46 / 23	8 / -5
December	38 / 17	3 / -8

Source: U.S. Climate Data; Period 1981-2010.

Table 3 – Average Temperatures at Lodgepole Campground (6,700 ft./2,042m)

Be aware that, while it may be sunny and hot during the day, as soon as the sun sets, temperatures can plummet rapidly. Keep this in mind when planning your arrival times at camp and when you might decide to bathe. The earlier you can set out in the morning, the more distance you can cover before the hottest part of the day and the more time you will have in camp to get washed up while the sun is still out and strong enough to dry and warm you.

Precipitation

In general, if you are hiking during late June to early September, you will have hot, clear weather at lower elevations and cold, clear weather at higher elevations. The amount of rain can vary from a brief downpour to a light drizzle over hours. Afternoon thunderstorms are not uncommon in the region but should pass fairly quickly. It is unlikely that you will encounter any snow during this time of year.

Table 4 below shows the average annual precipitation and snowfall at the Lodgepole Campground in Sequoia National Park (6,700ft/2,042m).

Month	Precipitation		Snowfall	
	(inch)	(mm)	(inch)	(cm)
Jan	8.35	212	46	117
Feb	8.43	214	52	132
Mar	6.85	174	41	104
Apr	3.27	83	20	51
May	1.42	36	5	13
Jun	0.63	16	1	3
Jul	0.63	16	0	0
Aug	0.28	7	0	0
Sep	0.98	25	0	0
Oct	2.24	57	3	8
Nov	4.72	120	15	38
Dec	7.64	194	36	91

Source: U.S. Climate Data; Period 1981-2010.

Table 4 – Average Precipitation and Snowfall at Lodgepole (6,700 ft./2,042m)

[!] When seeking shelter during a thunderstorm, move away from freestanding trees and place your pack and other metal objects at a distance. Avoid peaks and passes and stay low to the ground among scattered boulders or trees. You don't want to be the tallest thing around.

When I went in June 2014, the snowpack was exceptionally low and I ran into snow only in a couple of places. No special snow gear was necessary. That doesn't mean snow gear won't be necessary for you, but if you are traveling in late June to early September, it is unlikely you will have trouble with snow.

Before you leave on your trip, visit *www.forecast.weather.gov* and search for Sequoia National Park and Whitney Portal. This will give you an idea of the current expected weather at the beginning and ending points of your trip and help you determine whether you are likely to encounter any particularly severe conditions while you are on the trail. The website also features an interactive map that you can click on to get specific weather information for other areas along the HST.

d. Camping

This section covers the basics of campsites along the HST, including a list of well-established sites with distances and elevation figures as well as various rules and regulations you must follow in choosing and using campsites.

Figure 5 – Campsite at Upper Hamilton Lake

Regulations

In addition to the rules for what you can take with you on the HST and how you should use the trail, there are also rules for setting up and using campsites (see National Park Service website for details). Like the rules for trail use, these rules help minimize the impact that visitors have, keep the wilderness wild, and ensure that all visitors can enjoy their time on the HST safely.

General Camping Rules:

- No camping within 25 feet (8m) of water.
- Between 25-100 feet (8-30m) from water, you may only camp in previously well-established campsites.
- Camp only on durable surfaces (rock, sand, dirt, snow) or in designated campsites. Do not camp on vegetation or in meadows.
- Do not construct rock walls, trenches, or new fire rings.
- No camping within 2 miles (3.2km) of trailheads.
- Campfires are only allowed in certain areas (see section 'Campfires' below for details).

Area-Specific Campsite Restrictions:

- Camp only in designated spots at Bearpaw Meadow
- Two-night camping limit at Hamilton Lakes
- No camping at Timberline Lake (located before Guitar Lake)

Human Waste:

- Human waste must be buried at least 6 inches (15cm) deep and 200 feet (60m) from trails, campsites, and water sources.
- All toilet paper should be packed out in a waste bag.
- Inside the Whitney Zone (essentially covering Guitar Lake to Whitney Portal) you are not allowed to bury human waste. It, along with any toilet paper, must be packed out in a waste bag.

Food Storage:

- Food must be stored in an approved bear-resistant container. There are permanent bear boxes at most of the established campsites along the HST.
- Portable bear canisters are required once you reach Mt. Whitney, so you will need to bring your own canister to hold your food.

Campfires

Throughout Sequoia National Park, campfires are subject to restrictions and other requirements that hikers need to abide by at all times (see Table 5 below). Kings Canyon National Park also has rules in place, but these will not apply as long as you stay on the HST. Before embarking on your adventure, make sure to check the most current campfire restrictions as additional rules may be implemented during times of high fire danger.

Kaweah and Tule River Drainages (West of Great Western Divide)	Kern River Drainage (East of Great Western Divide)
• No fires anywhere above 9,000ft. • No fires in Hamilton Lakes Basin • No fires at Pinto Lake • No fires in Mineral King Valley above the ranger station • No fires in Summit Lake Basin • No fires in the Dillonwood area	• No fires anywhere above 10,400 ft. • No fires above 10,000 ft. at: Nine Lakes Basin, Big Arroyo, and within ¼ mile of the food storage box at Lower Crabtree Meadow
Other Requirements	
• Where fires are allowed, use existing fire rings. Do not build new ones or add rocks to existing fire rings. • Use only dead wood found on the ground. Do not chop live vegetation or remove dead branches from standing trees. • Fires must be attended at all times. • Do not burn trash. • Put out fires with water ½ hour before leaving your campsite and stir the ashes. Do not use dirt to put out fires.	

Table 5 – Overview of Campfire Restrictions and Requirements

Campfires are prohibited in the darkly shaded areas in Figure 6 below. Before you pass through Kaweah Gap (located after Hamilton Lakes but before Big Arroyo Junction), the campfire restrictions for the Kaweah and Tule River Drainages apply. Once you are past Kaweah Gap, the rules for the Sequoia National Park Kern River Drainage will apply.

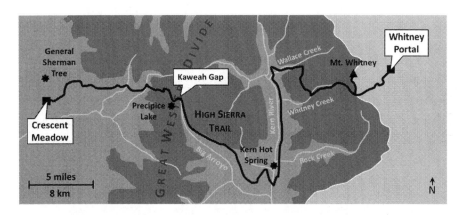

Figure 6 – Map of Allowed/Prohibited Campfire Locations

As a rule of thumb, unless you are absolutely certain that you are allowed to have a campfire, it is best not to start one. Many places on the HST will have existing fire rings at the campsites. However, the presence of a fire ring doesn't guarantee that fires are actually allowed.

⚠ Exercise extreme caution anytime you decide to make a campfire. Keep the fire small and use sticks no bigger than the size of one or two of your fingers together. Lighting a campfire in the wilderness is a great responsibility and can turn into a major disaster if not properly handled.

Established Campsites

There are a number of established campsites along the HST that you can use. When possible, you should always use an established campsite instead of making your own since this will be more convenient, more comfortable, and less damaging to the natural environment. Table 6 below provides an overview of all the campsites along the HST.[6]

Campsite	Distance from CM		Approx. Elevation		Bear Box avail.	Water avail.	Campfire OK
	miles	km	feet	meters			
Crescent Meadow (CM)	0.0	0.0	6,706	2,044	Yes	No	No
Mehrten Creek	6.5	10.5	7,635	2,327	Yes	Yes	Yes
9 Mile Creek	9.0	14.5	7,546	2,300	Yes	Yes	Yes
Buck Creek	10.5	16.9	7,200	2,195	Yes	Yes	Yes
Bearpaw Meadow	11.5	18.5	7,664	2,336	Yes	Yes	Yes
Lone Pine Creek	13.0	20.9	7,395	2,254	No	Yes	Yes
Upper Hamilton Lakes	16.5	26.6	8,238	2,511	Yes	Yes	No
Big Arroyo Junction	22.5	36.2	9,564	2,915	Yes	Yes	Yes
Moraine Lake	30.5	49.1	9,304	2,836	Yes	Yes	Yes
Upper Funston Meadow	34.5	55.5	6,650	2,027	Yes	Yes	Yes
Kern Hot Spring	37.0	59.6	6,916	2,108	Yes	Yes	Yes
Junction Meadow	44.0	70.8	8,074	2,461	Yes	Yes	Yes
Tyndall/Lake S. Am. Jct.	45.0	72.4	8,822	2,689	Yes	Yes	Yes
Wallace Creek	49.0	78.9	10,39	3,168	Yes	Yes	Yes
Crabtree Meadow	53.0	85.3	10,63	3,242	Yes	Yes	Yes
Guitar Lake	56.5	91.0	11,49	3,504	No	Yes	No
Trail Crest (west side)	61.5	99.0	13,43	4,096	No	No	No
Trail Camp	65.5	105.5	12,00	3,660	No	Yes	No
Outpost Camp	69.0	111.1	10,35	3,157	No	Yes	No
Whitney Portal	72.0	115.9	8,373	2,552	Yes	Yes	In camp

Table 6 – Overview of Established Campsites (distances rounded to nearest half mile)

---

[6] Elevation information retrieved from: *http://caltopo.com/m/232A*

Choosing a Wild Camping Site

Due to the number of established campsites found along the HST, it should be easy to plan your trip so that you're staying at a pre-existing campsite each night. If you find yourself camping in between sites or if you plan on taking off-trail side trips, consider the following factors when choosing a campsite:

Comfort – Avoid camping in basins and dips, where cold air will gather, and in close proximity to water. Moisture and dew can attract mosquitos, soak your gear, or cover it in frost. Moving just a few steps up and away from these areas can make for a much more comfortable night. At the same time, you want to have reasonably easy access to water for washing and cooking. Ideally, your campsite will also provide wind shelter while allowing the sun to shine brightly from the east to warm and dry your tent and sleeping bag in the morning. Choose dry sand or small gravel over any organic substance and vegetation to prevent moisture from creeping into your tent through the floor.

Strategy – Pick campsites that are convenient milestones for the distance and difficulty of each trail section. You will find that the existing campsites are often ideally located in this regard. Many are located just before particularly difficult sections of the trail, enabling you to tackle the most challenging portion of your day early on, while your legs are fresh and before it gets hot.

Impact on Nature – Minimizing your environmental impact helps preserve the trail and surrounding areas for fellow hikers and future generations. Here are a few basic principles you should follow when choosing a campsite (courtesy of the Leave No Trace Center for Outdoor Ethics):

- Camp on durable surfaces such as rock, gravel, sand, or snow. Avoid any type of vegetation if possible.
- Camp at very well established sites if available.
- Keep your campsite as small as possible.
- Camp at least 200 feet (60m) from lakes and streams.

- Camp in places that are suitable for camping as-is, i.e., you don't have to move rocks, branches, etc.

e. Water

The HST crosses numerous streams and skirts a number of year-round lakes, which means you should have no problem finding water during your trip. However, water sources will fluctuate depending on the season and whether there has been higher than average precipitation or a drought. Expect more in spring and early summer as the snowmelt and seasonal rains swell the creeks. Expect less in fall as you reach the driest part of the year before the winter storms come.

Kern River

As of the writing of this book, California is in the midst of a very significant drought that has lasted for several years. Average snowpack has been far below normal, which translates into less water flowing through the waterways and for a shorter period of time. It is advisable to plan out your water resupply points to make sure you are carrying enough to drink throughout the day, but not so much that it adds unnecessary weight to your pack.

 As a rule of thumb, the average hiker will consume approx. one gallon of water per day, including meal preparation.

Maps vs. Reality – When planning your water consumption and resupply strategy, be aware that just because your map has a little blue line indicating a river or stream, it does not mean that reality will cooperate with your map. Smaller rivers and streams may be seasonal in nature and should therefore be viewed as sources where water *might be* rather than *will be*. Major drainages fed by many tributary streams should be more likely to have water in them than the small tributary streams. Similarly, large lakes are more likely to have water in them than small ponds which may be seasonal as well.

Quality

Most, if not all, of the water along the HST will be snowmelt, making it cool in temperature and of good quality. It's best to get your water from sources that are moving and deep (such as streams), rather than shallow stagnant water (ponds and puddles). There are plenty of streams along the HST that will meet your needs.

(i) I prefer to get my water from streams and 50 feet (15m) or so upstream from any trail crossings, thereby further reducing the likelihood that it has been contaminated by other humans.

Regardless of where you get your water on the HST and how clean it may appear, it should still be filtered and treated prior to consumption. Any water coming from natural sources could potentially be contaminated with waterborne parasites or bacteria, such as Protozoan Giardia lamblia and E.coli. They can cause diarrhea and abdominal cramps, even 5-15 days after exposure. Fortunately, both can be filtered out and/or killed with common treatment methods, which are discussed further in Section 6d *Food & Water*. Since it is impossible to know for sure if that water you're about to drink is contaminated or not, better to play it safe and filter all the water you drink.

Washing

The HST is a 72-mile trek through the wilderness. You're going to be sweaty and dirty *every night*. Given the remoteness of the trail, there are no facilities to wash yourself, your clothes or equipment. When you feel too dirty to bear, you will have to find a lake, strip those clothes off, jump in, give yourself a good rub, get out and get on with things. It's all part of the experience.

In order to avoid contaminating water sources, keep a distance of 100 feet (30m) when using any kind of soap to wash yourself, your clothing, or your cooking utensils. Use bio-degradable soap or, ideally, refrain from using any kind of detergent altogether. Leftover food and human waste should be buried at least 6 inches (15cm) deep and 200 feet (60m) away from water sources, trails, and campsites.

Being solo, I wasn't very convinced that there was much to be gained by being soap-level clean, so I didn't take any. The thought of spending time washing stuff just wasn't very appealing, nor was the thought of carrying additional weight and/or having an extra piece of clutter to keep track of. Regardless of what you decide, take what you need in order to meet only your most basic hygiene requirements. If you can stand being a little dirty, ditching your toiletries is a great way to reduce your pack weight.

f. Safety

Safety is an important part of any trip, but even more so when you are hiking through the wilderness where it will be difficult to get help during an emergency. Safety on the HST means, among other things, that you are well prepared for the hike, have the right gear, are in good physical shape, understand how to avoid dangerous situations, and are prepared to deal with dangerous situations if they arise. Different people may define safety differently, but everyone should understand the risks of a long hike through the mountains before they decide to hit the trail.

Travel

Being located in the United States, traveling to and from the HST is probably not as significant a safety concern as it could be in other parts of the world. Even so, you should still exercise caution in getting to and from the trailheads and understand the risks of what you are doing. This is particularly true if you decide to hitchhike. It is relatively common for hikers to hitchhike from Whitney Portal down to the town of Lone Pine in order to link up with other transportation. Personally, I would not feel comfortable hitchhiking any portions of my trip other than Whitney Portal to Lone Pine. Whether you decide to hitchhike and for what portions of your trip is ultimately up to you and at your own risk.

Both trailheads are relatively high traffic, meaning that there should be people around them most of the time during the day. I've always considered this a good thing since I think having more people around decreases the chances of anyone messing with me or my car. If you are parking a car at one or both of the trailheads, make sure you do not leave any valuables in the car and nothing in sight that would encourage someone to try breaking into it. If you're like me, there is almost nowhere I feel safer than when surrounded by hikers and campers.

Bears are not uncommon at either trailhead. Unfortunately, bears do not have car insurance and are notoriously bad for reporting "accidents". This means that when they tear your door to pieces to find out what's inside that cooler on your backseat, chances are good that they are not going to wait around until you get back to your car and help you file the police report. Do not leave any food in your car and do not leave any coolers visible. Bears know what coolers look like and are more than willing to do some work to find out what's inside yours.

Camping

Before you pitch your tent at night, it's a good idea to take a look at your surroundings to make sure you're not pitching it on top of an anthill or next to a dead tree that could potentially fall over. Animals, such as rodents and bears, shouldn't be too interested in you unless you have food in your tent or you smell like food. Best practices are to never take anything scented into the tent with you at night. This means no food, no drinks other than water, no delicious-tasting lip balms, etc. If you cooked anything particularly pungent or spilled food on your clothes, you might also want to consider leaving them outside your tent in the vestibule or elsewhere. Make sure all your food is in your bear canister and both your canister and clothes are secured to something so an animal doesn't run off with them. Pile rocks on top of them, bury them in the dirt, wedge them into trees, etc.

Bears

It would not be uncommon to see bears in this part of the Sierra. Black bears are the only species of bears found in the wild in California. Despite their name, their color can range from black to a cinnamon brown, the latter being more common in California. Here are a few ways to increase your chances of not running into a bear on the HST:

- Make noise when you're walking. Consider taking a bear bell and make a point of singing, talking, banging your hiking poles together every so often, etc. just to give the rest of nature some advanced notice that you are coming its way.
- Don't keep any food or other scented items inside your tent.
- Use the bear canister that you are required to take with you and put it at least 30 ft. (9m) from your tent at night.
- Use the permanent bear boxes in addition to the canisters when they are available. If you're not familiar, bear boxes are large steel containers with locking doors that bears can't open. Most of the campsites along the HST will have these.

⚠ Refer to the National Park Service website for additional advice on how to deal with the situation in case you do encounter a black bear and remember that bear spray is not allowed on the HST.

Snakes

Figure 7 – Rattlesnake in Kern River Valley

Rattlesnakes inhabit many regions of California and can live at elevations up to around 10,000 ft. (3,048m). While this means that you have the potential to run into rattlesnakes during most of the HST, you are more likely to find them in the warmer, lower elevation portions of the trail, like Sequoia National Park and the Kern River Basin. The main thing you want to avoid is startling them. This includes stepping on them, stepping near them, or otherwise coming into close proximity. Rattlesnakes can sense you coming through the vibrations in the ground and are likely to get out of the way, provided they have enough time to do so. They don't want to run into you any more than you want to run into them. Here are a few tips to help you avoid a bad encounter with a rattlesnake:

- Only step where you can clearly see the ground. This means that you shouldn't be stepping into bushes or tall grass, over logs or rocks, or otherwise placing your feet anywhere you can't see beforehand.
- Don't stick your hands anywhere you can't see. Fortunately, there are few if any places on the HST where your hands will need to be involved in moving you, so you won't often find yourself putting your hands in places where a rattlesnake could be sitting.
- If you have to step somewhere you can't see (e.g., while wading through a dense underbrush of ferns), it's a good idea to walk slowly, stomp your feet, and use your hiking poles to probe at the path in front of you before stepping forward.

[!] You can find more information about how to avoid and deal with rattlesnakes here: *https://www.wildlife.ca.gov/News/Snake*

Altitude Sickness

You'll have several days where you ascend and descend thousands of feet and reach elevations as high as 14,505 ft. (4,421m) at the summit of Mt. Whitney. At these elevations, it is very possible that you could succumb to altitude sickness, which occurs when you cannot get enough oxygen from the "thinner" air at high altitudes. This causes symptoms such as a headache, loss of appetite, and trouble sleeping. It happens most often when people who are not used to oxygen-deficient air go quickly from lower elevations to 8000 ft. (2438m) or higher. It is recommended that HST hikers understand the symptoms of altitude sickness and are prepared to deal with it.

Fear of Heights

If you are afraid of heights, I would recommend that you be honest with yourself about this before you go on the trail. If you don't know whether you are, the trail is going to give you a couple of chances to find out. Although this is a walking trail and not some rock-climbing adventure, there are a few points along this trail where people who are particularly afraid of heights may be less than comfortable. (Full disclosure, two of my family members are very afraid of heights, so I am perhaps a bit more sensitive to this possible issue than most.)

The trail has some narrow sections with steep drop-offs in the first two days, so you will be able to test yourself early on. Arguably the most "exciting" section of the trail in this regard will be on day two or three, as you pass through Hamilton Gorge before you reach Kaweah Gap. In 1938, after an avalanche had torn out the bridge the year before, the Civilian Conservation Corps blasted a ledge trail and tunnel through the rock to reconnect the trail along this section. If you get past Hamilton Gorge, you should have absolutely no issues until at least the ascent and decent of Mt. Whitney several days later (at which point you will have little choice but soldier on rather than bail out and head back to the start - problem solved!).

General Precautions

Whether you are hiking solo or with a buddy, it is always a good idea to inform a third party about your detailed hiking plans. Be aware that cell phone reception is limited along the HST. Carrying a simple whistle will increase your chances of getting help sooner in case of emergency. Some hikers may even opt to bring a satellite-based emergency device along.

g. Flora & Fauna

The HST will bring you face to face with some truly stunning features of the natural world. This short section doesn't begin to do justice to all that you will see on the trail. If you are interested in learning more, there are a number of books and online resources that will provide far more information than this book will be able to cover. Recommendations for additional reading are provided in the *Links & References* section of the Appendix.

The Sierra Nevada owe their impressive granite cliffs and plunging, U-shaped valleys to a combination of glacial and tectonic forces that have been sculpting this masterpiece for millions of years. Over the course of the HST, you will be treated to some awe-inspiring examples of these forces at work. Valhalla and the Angels Wings are two stunning sights in the area surrounding the Hamilton Lake Basin that are worth a moment of silence, as are the sheer rock wall behind Precipice Lake and the east face of Mt. Whitney.

Figure 8 – Sheer Rock Wall behind Precipice Lake

As striking as the geology of the HST may be, it would hard to rank it as the most impressive natural feature you will see on this trip. That honor can only belong to the giant sequoias, the largest trees in the world. You will see a number of these trees as you make your way to the Lodgepole Visitor

Center to pick up your permit. Before you take off on the HST, be sure to make a stop to see the General Sherman Tree, the largest of the giant sequoias, which has earned it the distinction as the largest tree in the world (by volume). The General Sherman Tree is conveniently located a short distance off the road that you have to take to go from Lodgepole to the trailhead at Crescent Meadow.

Sequoia National Park is home to a wide variety of plants and animals. The park can be broadly divided into three climate zones: Foothills (below 4,500 ft.), Montane (4,500 ft. - 9,000 ft.), and Alpine (above 9,000 ft.). Each of these zones supports a different ecosystem with its own diverse selection of plants and animals. The HST passes only through the Montane and Alpine zones.

The following are some of the most common plants that you are likely to see along the HST:

- Ponderosa pine
- Incense cedar
- White fir
- Red fir

- Sugar pine
- Lodgepole pine
- Foxtail pine
- Snow plant

Figure 9 – Snow Plant (Sarcodes sanguinea)

You should not encounter any floral hazards along the HST. In case this needs to be said, refrain from eating any plants that you do not specifically know are OK to eat. Unless you have studied the plants of this region extensively and consider yourself a very competent botanist in this regard, don't eat anything on the HST.

The following are some of the most common mammals that you are likely to see along the HST:

- Black bear
- Mule deer
- Yellow-bellied marmot

- Ground squirrels
- Chipmunks
- Clark's nutcracker

Figure 10 – Deer in Meadow

If you're lucky, you may even spot bighorn sheep or mountain lions, but sightings are rare. There are a few areas in particular where you will likely have animals trying to scavenge your food: Hamilton Lakes and the area around Mt. Whitney. Why these two places? The simple answer is that these are the two areas with the highest people traffic on the HST. Over time, animals have become more accustomed to people and have gotten used to finding (or being fed) people food. They're less timid and are more willing to risk getting close in order to find out what goodies are inside your backpack.

Fortunately, most of the fauna along the HST are not so used to people that they are likely to approach you. It will be your responsibility to help keep things this way. If you do encounter any wildlife, remember that feeding them is illegal. In addition, feeding wild animals can indeed be very harmful to them. Besides the fact that they did not evolve to eat our food, feeding animals will encourage them to approach people in the future. Over time, this can increase their dependency on people for food and decrease their natural food gathering abilities. It also creates a constant nuisance for future hikers as they have to do more to protect their supplies.

When you're not actively pulling something out of your bear canister or putting something in it, put the lid on and give it a couple of turns. You don't have to lock it down if you're going to use it again, just make sure to put the lid on so you don't let some ninja rodent take off with the dinner that you're going to need later in your trip.

h. Other Conditions

Wildfires

Any hike in the Sierras presents the potential to encounter wildfires. If there are wildfires anywhere in the region before your trip, make sure they have no potential to put you in harm's way. Before you set out, call the ranger station at the Lodgepole Visitors Center in Sequoia National Park (near the start) and the station in Lone Pine (near the end) to check hiking conditions and any trail closures. If there's any indication that a portion of the trail could be even remotely at risk from a wildfire, it's better to look for an alternate start date after the wildfire threat has been eliminated.

Rockslides & Flash Floods

You will be hiking in mountainous areas where landslides or rockslides could be triggered by earthquakes, melting snow, human activity, or other factors. You can help protect yourself and those you are traveling with by being alert, staying on the trail, and avoiding being directly underneath or above other hikers. If you see a falling rock, yell "ROCK" at the top of your lungs to alert other hikers as quickly as possible to the potential threat. If you're hiking in or near a riverbed and the water turns from clear to muddy or the water level begins to rise, get to high ground immediately as these could be indications of a flash flood further upstream.

Strikes & Government Shutdowns

Although unlikely, there is always a potential that strikes or government shutdowns could affect your travel and hiking plans. Always check to make sure that your public transportation is running as expected and that the park entrance is open before you set off on your trip.

4. Long Lead Items

Choosing the date on which you will hit the trail and the total duration of your hike will be a critical and influential step in your journey. Once you've decided on a particular schedule, it will begin to dictate all other planning activities you need to complete before you set off on your adventure. The items discussed in this chapter have significant implications for your schedule and require sufficient lead time. It is a good idea to take care of these early on in the planning process.

a. Permits & Regulations

Like many popular trails in the Sierra Nevada, the National Park Service has implemented a quota system during a portion of the year to limit the number of people using the trails for overnight trips in Sequoia and Kings Canyon National Parks. For the HST, there are two types of wilderness permits – one for inside the quota period and one for outside the quota period. As of the writing of this book, the quota period is May 22 to September 26. From September 27 to May 21 there is no quota. As these details are subject to change, be sure to check the National Park Service website for most current quota dates and information for the year you plan to go.

Since the vast majority of people will hike the HST inside the quota period (and I recommend you do as well), this section will focus on permits for inside the quota period.

Quota Period: May 22 - September 26

During the quota period, the National Park Service limits the number of people that can enter the HST to a maximum of 30 per day. If you plan to start your hike during this time, you will be required to apply for a wilderness permit by filling out an application form and paying a non-refundable application fee of $15. If you start your hike outside of the quota period, there is no limit to the number of people who can embark on the HST, and wilderness permits are free of charge and self-issued at the Lodgepole Visitor Center.

! In choosing when to hike, remember that while starting during the quota period means you'll have to go through an application process and pay a fee, going outside of the quota period may mean that you'll have to deal with snow which may be difficult or even impossible to pass in certain areas.

Validity of Permit

Permits for the HST only matter for the starting point of your trip and the day on which you plan to enter the trail. The National Park Service uses your entry point to control the number of people on the trail at a given time. Once you are on the trail, you can change where and when you will end your trip. This is useful if you decide to extend your trip and/or exit somewhere other than Whitney Portal.

Permits can be reserved for a maximum group size of 15 people. It should be noted, however, that due to the limited number of permits issued each day, the larger your group the more likely that you may have trouble finding a day with enough space left in the quota to accommodate your group.

Application Process

From the 30 permits issued per day during the quota season, three quarters can be reserved in advance. The remaining one quarter is given out on a first-come, first-served basis at the Lodgepole Visitor Center. Permit reservations are accepted each year beginning at *midnight on March 1*. You must submit your application at least two weeks before your intended start date. I recommend you submit as far in advance as possible to maximize your chances of getting a permit. Applications can only be submitted via mail or fax (no emails). The mailing address and fax number are listed on the permit application form, which you can download from the National Park Service website.

When filling out your application, make sure to complete all required fields before submitting it. In the trip information section, put "High Sierra" for the entry trail and "Whitney Portal" for your exit trail (or any other exit route you plan on taking). The exit trail matters much less than the entry point, and you can change your exit route before or during your hike without penalty. Similarly, your exit dates matter much less than your entry dates. Your entry dates will be locked in once your permit is approved, but you can adjust your exit dates before or during your trip.

Here is an example of a completed trip information section on the permit application:

	Entry Date	Entry Trail	Exit Date	Exit Trail
1	June 6	High Sierra	June 13	Whitney Portal
2	July 3	High Sierra	July 11	Whitney Portal
3	July 8	High Sierra	July 15	Whitney Portal
4	July 12	High Sierra	July 19	Whitney Portal

Preferred # of people in group: 6   **Min. # of people acceptable:** 4

Table 7 – Sample Wilderness Permit Application (Trip Information Section)

In the above example, the submitter provided four entry dates, with June 6 being their first choice. Further, they indicated that they would like a permit for a group of six but would accept a permit for a group of four if there isn't enough room for a group of six. When the Park Service receives the application, they will check to see whether the first choice is available. If it is, great news, the submitter gets exactly what they asked for. If there isn't room for the preferred minimum party size (4) on the first choice entry date (June 6), they will proceed to the second choice and so on until they either find a start date that meets the criteria specified or get to the end of the list. If no dates are available which meet the minimum criteria, no permit will be reserved.

Important information about completing your permit application:

- Complete all required fields before submitting your application.
- You must submit your payment (if paying by check or money order) or payment information (if paying by credit card) at the time you apply.
- Within two weeks of them receiving your application, you will receive an email confirmation *only if* your application was processed successfully.
- The email confirmation *is not your permit*. You must bring a printed copy of the email to pick up your actual permit.

! Permit applications are reviewed in the order they are received. No notification is given to those who *do not* get a permit. The permit office recommends that if you haven't heard back within two weeks of submitting your permit, submit again for a different combination of days and/or group sizes.

Permit Pickup

Permits for the HST are issued *only* at the Lodgepole Visitor Center in Sequoia National Park:

Lodgepole Visitor Center
63100 Lodgepole Rd
Sequoia National Park, CA 93262
Phone: +1 (559) 565-4436

The group leader (identified on the application) must be present to pick up the permit. They will need to bring a printout of the confirmation email. The permit must be picked up either after 1pm the day before the hike or before 9am on the morning of the entry date. If the permit is not picked up by 9am, the respective permit spots will be given to walk-ins. If you need to arrange for a late pick up, call or email the Park Service Wilderness Office (Phone: +1 (559) 565-3766 *or* E-mail: seki_wilderness_office@nps.gov) and see instructions on the permit application.

! Since the group leader who submitted the application must be present to pick up the permit, do not trust anyone who is selling a permit for the HST online.

You will need to have an approved bear canister with you on the HST. Due to the duration of the trip, it is highly likely that each member of your party will need to have their own bear canister to take all the food they will need.

Permit Strategy

Here are some tips for maximizing your chances of getting a permit for the days and size of group you are requesting:

Submit early!

Ideally, you want to submit your permit as early as possible. The longer you wait, the more likely that permits will no longer be available for your preferred days. Reservations open at midnight on March 1. I recommend you submit your application via fax on March 2 (see below for further explanation). Quotas for popular days (weekends/holidays) and times of year (summer months) can fill up quickly.

! If you submit before midnight of March 1, your application *will not be processed*. This is why I recommend you submit on March 2, just to be sure that you don't end up getting it there too early. I recommend using the fax method, because you'll get a confirmation that your application arrived on the day you intended.[7]

Keep your group size small.

The smaller your group size, the more likely that there will still be spots for you. I recommend keeping your application to four people or fewer. Although the Park Service can issue 30 permits per day, only three quarters can be reserved in advance.

---

[7] If you don't have access to a fax machine, there are free online fax services that are easy to set up and simple to use.

Provide multiple alternative entry days.

The permit application will allow you to submit up to four alternatives for starting days and trails (see Table 7 on page 38). The Park Service will issue your permit for the first day that is available based on the order you list your alternatives.

Check availability before submitting.

Before submitting your application, check the wilderness permit availability for the HST and the days you would like to travel on the National Park Service website (section "Trailhead Availability"). This will prevent you from submitting an application for a group size and day that is already fully booked.

b. Hiking Buddy

Early in your planning process, you will need to decide whether you are hiking alone or with a group. If you are going with a group, the decision on how many people are going can have a wide variety of implications, including when you can hike (accommodating everyone's schedules), how many people to put on your permit application, travel options, shared gear options, and how to divvy up the planning workload. As you might imagine or have already experienced, hiking solo has certain advantages and disadvantages. Below is a short list of some considerations.

Arguments *for* Hiking Solo

The trip you're planning will actually happen.

If you're prepared to go solo, but don't end up going, you have only one person to blame. For me, planning for solo trips has meant that I spend my time preparing for my trip, rather than spending my time trying to convince others to join and/or coordinate their attendance, only to be disappointed when someone drops out at the last minute. I'm also not stuck scrambling last minute to rearrange my travel plans or my gear list if someone decides not to join. I now invite people to join me, but plan my trips expecting that I might have to go solo.

It's entirely up to you.

You answer only to yourself. If you want to do something, you do it. If you don't want to do something, you don't do it. It's as simple as that. Going solo means that you camp where and when you want, eat where and when you want, and hike where and at the pace you want. This has helped me understand my limitations, desires, and capabilities without the influence of others. I have never felt more genuinely free and in touch with myself than when hiking alone.

You set the hiking pace.

In general, going with a buddy will never be faster than going alone. They need a pee break when you don't. You need a rest break when they don't. They want to take a picture of another "stunning vista" that to you looks just like the last fourteen stunning vistas you passed and all you can think of is mac and cheese and taking off your boots.

No compromising needed.

Coordinating a group of people with varying levels of outdoor experience, physical fitness, vacation times, budgets, and general interests can present a huge challenge in itself. If you are not the type of person who's able/willing to assume or delegate the extra responsibility to accommodate different, potentially conflicting opinions and schedules, you are probably better off planning a solo trip.

What happens when you don't have to talk or listen.

Being alone on the trail for several days was an amazing experience. It allowed me to get into my own head, free of the constant white noise that comes with being around other people. A solo hike on the HST was like seven days of silent meditation in the wilderness, interrupted only occasionally by a passerby. If this level of solitude does not sound appealing, be sure to bring a hiking buddy.

Arguments *against* Hiking Solo

Fewer safety nets.

If you run out of food, there will be no one around to help you out. If you twist your ankle, you're going to be really good at hobbling by the time you get off of the trail. Any situation that's already precarious for a group of two or more people can have serious consequences for a group of one. If you aren't the most experienced hiker, the duration and physical requirements of the HST might not be the best place to put your self-reliance to the test.

You carry everything.

When traveling with others, you can reduce the group's total pack weight by sharing certain items, such as a tent, stove, water filter, first aid kit, and maps. Solo hiking does not give you this luxury. Everything you want to take on the HST will be on your back at the Crescent Meadow trailhead. You can help compensate for this by being more disciplined about taking only the essential gear and upgrading your gear to more "ultralight" type options.

Greater logistical effort.

If you're hiking with a group of people with more than one car at their disposal, you can drop one car at Whitney Portal, where you will end your hike, and then use the other car to get to the trailhead at Crescent Meadow. Even if there is only one car or none at all, travelling as a group could help split some of the costs for transportation/shuttle services.

No second opinion.

Having a hiking partner can offer a peace of mind and confidence that you may want out there in the wild. Should you push on a little further or call it a day? Should you skip this water opportunity and head for the next? It's getting pretty late, should you get down off this mountain now so you get to camp before dark? What was that noise? Having a sounding board and a second opinion can provide a lot of assurance when you're making decisions and dealing with situations on the trail. If you think you'd like a second set of hands and eyes, make sure you to bring along a friend.

Memories and the shared experience.

Sharing the experience with someone may have intrinsic value. You're going to see a lot of amazing things on this trip. Those memories and the stories that you will tell your friends may be richer if shared with someone else who will be able to relate. Although I went solo, I was able to mitigate the loss of the "shared experience" to a certain degree by recording a lot of my hike on camera, which I then compiled to share with friends and family. It's never going to be the same as having someone with you, but it's better than nothing.

c. Travel Arrangements

You will need to arrange transportation to the trailhead at Crescent Meadow and again from Whitney Portal where you will end your hike. This book provides options for two potential starting points, San Francisco and Los Angeles, both of which have major airports and public transportation options. If you plan on traveling to and from the trailheads using public transportation, Los Angeles is a cheaper and much faster starting/ending point for your trip

Transportation Options to/from Trailheads

There are several ways to get to and from the starting and ending points of the HST, regardless of whether you start your trip in San Francisco or Los Angeles. These options can be combined in a number of ways to suit your individual travel needs, schedule, and budget.

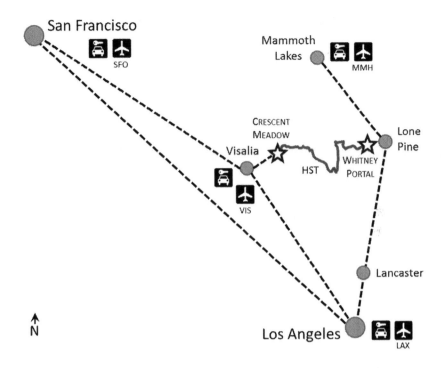

Figure 11 – Overview of Travel Options

Drop-off and Pickup by Family and Friends

If you can arrange it, this is probably the best option for getting to and from the HST, since it eliminates the time for dropping off and retrieving cars before and after your trip as well as the hassle of having to coordinate public transportation. Maybe you have a family member or friend who is willing to do it for free or for gas money. Even if it takes a bit more "incentive" to get them to agree, it will likely still be the cheapest and most convenient option.

Personal Car(s) & Parking

Both Crescent Meadow and Whitney Portal have parking lots where you can leave cars for the duration of your trip. If you are hiking the HST with a friend and you both have cars, you can drive to Whitney Portal, leave one car there, and then use the other car to get to the trailhead at Crescent

Meadow. At the end of your hike, you will obviously need to drive back to the Crescent Meadow trailhead to pick up the car you left there.

If you are hiking the HST alone or only have one car between all the people in your group, you can drive that car to Whitney Portal, leave it at the trailhead, and then get transportation to the trailhead in Crescent Meadow. Since it's hard to predict what time of day or night you will arrive at the end of your hike, leaving your car at Whitney Portal gives you flexibility to immediately start your trip home or head into town to stay for the night.

! Since you *must be on time* to pick up your permit from the Lodgepole Visitor Center, if you decide to leave your car at Whitney Portal, make sure you understand how you are going to get to the permit office and how long it is going to take you.

There is bear activity at both trailheads, which means that you should cover up any food and/or coolers in your car so that they are not visible to bears. Unless you absolutely must have food in your car, I would recommend against it to minimize the likelihood of coming back to a bear-induced crime scene of mangled auto parts and food wrappers.

i As a precaution, I like to leave a note on my car dashboard indicating the starting date of my trip, the trail I will be on, and my expected return date. This serves two purposes: First, park rangers will know that my car will be there for a while, and second, if my expected return date has come and gone and my car is still there, it can alert them that I could be in trouble.

If there is not enough room in the Whitney Portal parking lot, you may want to contact the *Dow Villa Motel* in Lone Pine to see if you can arrange for long-term parking there (see Appendix H for contact information).

Public Transportation

Bay Area Rapid Transit (BART)

Regional rail service that will take you from San Francisco International Airport (SFO) to the city of Richmond, CA, where you can link up with Amtrak trains for longer distance travel throughout California.

Approximate cost: *$10*   Website: *http://www.bart.gov*

Amtrak

Major railroad carrier in California used for long trips between cities. You can take this carrier to get from Los Angeles or San Francisco to the city of Visalia, CA, for the start of the trip and from the city of Lancaster, CA, back to San Francisco at the end of your trip.

Approximate cost: *$35-$65*   Website: *http://www.amtrak.com*

Metrolink

Regional passenger rail system serving Southern California. You can take this carrier to get from the city of Lancaster, CA, back to Los Angeles at the end of your trip.

Approximate cost: *$15*   Website: h*ttp://www.metrolinktrains.com*

Sequoia Shuttle

Travels between the city of Visalia, CA, and Sequoia National Park. Shuttle also operates several routes inside the park that you can use to get your permit and get to the starting trailhead of the HST. Reservations are required.

Approximate cost: *$15*   Website: *http://www.sequoiashuttle.com*

Megabus

Long-distance bus service. Megabus can transport you between Los Angeles and San Francisco and is generally less expensive than traveling by train, however, route options are limited.

Approximate cost: *$40*   Website: *http://us.megabus.com*

Eastern Sierra Transit Authority (ESTA)

Bus service traveling along Highway 395. You can use ESTA to north or south from the city of Lone Pine, CA, which is located ca. 11 miles from the ending trailhead at Whitney Portal.

Approximate cost: *$25-$50*   Website: *http://www.estransit.com*

FlyAway Bus

Bus services that will take you to and from Los Angeles International Airport (LAX) and Union Station, the major train station in Los Angeles. You will need to print your reservation and bring it with you. Tickets are valid for 30 days after the date of purchase.

Approximate cost: *$8*   Website: *http://www.lawa.org/FlyAway/*

Below are sample itineraries indicating possible connections from the two major hubs (LAX, SFO) to the start of the trail and back (incl. approx. cost):

From	To	Transportation	Cost
SFO	Richmond, CA	BART	$10
Richmond, CA	Visalia, CA	Amtrak	$42
Visalia, CA	Sequoia NP (Giant Forest Museum)	Sequoia Shuttle	$15
Sequoia NP (Giant Forest Museum)	Lodgepole Visitor Center	Sequoia Shuttle	
Lodgepole Visitor Center	**Crescent Meadow**	Sequoia Shuttle	
Total			**$67**

Table 8 – Sample Itinerary: SFO to Crescent Meadow

From	To	Transportation	Cost
LAX	L.A. Union Station	FlyAway Bus	$8
L.A. Union Station	Visalia, CA	Amtrak	$35
Visalia, CA	Sequoia NP (Giant Forest Museum)	Sequoia Shuttle	$15
Sequoia NP (Giant Forest Museum)	Lodgepole Visitor Center	Sequoia Shuttle	
Lodgepole Visitor Center	**Crescent Meadow**	Sequoia Shuttle	
Total			**$58**

Table 9 – Sample Itinerary: LAX to Crescent Meadow

From	To	Transport.	Cost
Whitney Portal	Lone Pine, CA	see note below	-
Lone Pine, CA	Lancaster, CA	ESTA	$25
Lancaster, CA	L.A. Union Station	Metrolink	$15
L.A. Union Station	West Oakland (BART Station)	Megabus	$10-$40
West Oakland (BART Station)	**SFO**	BART	$10
Total			**$60-$90**

Table 10 – Sample Itinerary: Whitney Portal to SFO

From	To	Transportation	Cost
Whitney Portal	Lone Pine, CA	see note below	-
Lone Pine, CA	Lancaster, CA	ESTA	$25
Lancaster, CA	L.A. Union Station	Metrolink	$15
L.A. Union Station	**LAX**	FlyAway Bus	$8
Total			**$48**

Table 11 – Sample Itinerary: Whitney Portal to LAX

Note: As of the writing of this book, there is no public transportation available to get from Whitney Portal to the town of Lone Pine 11.4 miles (18.4km) away, which is the nearest point where you will find public transportation. While there are no guarantees, the amount of hikers and campers that are arriving and departing from Whitney Portal means you can probably find someone who would be willing to take you down the mountain to Lone Pine. Whether you are comfortable hitchhiking or not is entirely up to you and should only ever be done with appropriate care and precaution. Alternatively, you could arrange for a private shuttle service or individual to come and pick you up.

Private Shuttle Service/Chartered Transportation

<u>Eastern Sierra Shuttle</u>

This company offers chartered private rides that you can book in advance and customize to your particular needs. Rates depend on the number of people in your party. While not necessarily cheap, this may be your best option for getting from Whitney Portal back to where you will depart for home. You can, for instance, hire them to take you from Whitney Portal back to the Crescent Meadow trailhead where you may have parked a car. Or perhaps you took public transportation to the trailhead in Crescent Meadow, you can then use the shuttle service to get you from Whitney Portal to Lone Pine, the closest connection to public transportation. Contact them to find out more about your options and to make travel reservations.

Website: *http://www.eastsidesierrashuttle.com*

<u>Climber.org</u>

You can check the "shuttles" section of this online community for additional information about potential transportation options to and from Whitney Portal and other trailheads in the region.

Website: *http://www.climber.org/data/shuttles.html*

Mule Post

You may be able to arrange for a rideshare or alternative transportation on this local classified ads website (similar to Craigslist), which caters to the community of the Eastern Sierra Nevada.

Website: *http://mulepost.com/community/ride-share*

Taxi/Rideshare Services & Car Rental

Taxis and rideshare services, such as Uber and Lyft, are also options for getting to and from the trailhead or for particular segments where other means of transportation are too inconvenient. Check cost and availability before relying on either of these, since much of your travel will be in remote areas that may or may not be easy accessible and have limited cell phone reception to make calls.

Car rental options will be available in many of the larger cities in California, including Visalia, near the start, and Ridgecrest, near the end. Cars can usually be rented for one-way trips, enabling you, for example, to rent a car in Ridgecrest and leave it at LAX if desired.

Regional Airports

You may also consider flying to regional airports that are closer to the starting and ending trailheads:

Crescent Meadow (~60 miles)	Whitney Portal (~110 miles)
Visalia Municipal Airport (VIS) 9501 W Airport Dr. Visalia, CA 93277 Phone: +1 (559) 713-4201	Mammoth Yosemite Airport (MMH) 1200 Airport Road Mammoth Lakes, CA 93546 Phone: +1 (760) 934-3813
Departing from: Los Angeles (LAX), Burbank (BUR)	*Arriving at:* Los Angeles (LAX), San Francisco (SFO)
Carriers: Alaska Airlines, American Airlines	*Carriers:* Alaska Airlines, American Airlines, United Airlines

Table 12 – Regional Airports Closest to Trailheads

If you do decide to fly, keep in mind that you will still need to arrange for transportation to and from these regional airports using one or more of the other options provided in this section.

d. Accommodation

While there are virtually no accommodations along the HST, there are some options near the starting and ending trailheads. If you would like to upgrade your backcountry experience, consider spending a night at one of the lodges or special seasonal camps in Sequoia National Park.

ⓘ Be aware that due to the popularity of Sequoia National Park and Mt. Whitney, campsites and other accommodation options usually sell out far in advance, so it is best to book as early as possible.

Before the HST

There are several campgrounds and other lodging options inside Sequoia National Park. You may be able to reserve some campsites in advance while others will be given out on a first-come, first-served basis. Camping or staying inside the park has the benefit of helping you get acclimated to the higher elevation before you set out. Rates may significantly vary depending on the dates you choose to stay.

Camping in Sequoia:

http://www.nps.gov/seki/planyourvisit/campgrounds.htm

Hotel and other lodging options in Sequoia:

http://www.visitsequoia.com/reservations.aspx

Alternatively, and particularly if you are taking the Sequoia Shuttle to get into the park, you can stay in the town of Visalia. The shuttle departs from several different locations in Visalia, many of which are hotels. Simply search online to pick from a variety of options. Before you book, don't forget to call the hotel to confirm that the Sequoia Shuttle will actually pick you up from their location.

After the HST

There are a number of campsites around Whitney Portal that you can try and reserve ahead of time. Alternately, you can book other accommodations in the town of Lone Pine, which you will need to pass through on your way back home. Rates may vary significantly depending on the dates you choose to stay.

Camping at Whitney Portal:

http://www.recreation.gov (search for 'Whitney Portal')

High Sierra Camps

High Sierra Camps offer a more "luxurious" wilderness camping experience by providing cozy tent cabins, hot showers, and hearty meals. The camps are open seasonally, usually from early June to late September (varies by year), and reservation is required. There are two camps just off the HST - Sequoia High Sierra Camp and Bearpaw High Sierra Camp.

Just a short hike (less than a mile) from the starting trailhead, *Sequoia High Sierra Camp* offers 32 canvas tented cabins and a rather upscale camping experience. *Bearpaw High Sierra Camp* is located near mile 11.5 of the HST and offers a more basic experience with its six tent cabins. Despite its smaller size and more rustic character, guests still enjoy a wide range of amenities, including a full-time staff. For more information about each camp's amenities, reservation policy, and rates, refer to their respective websites:

Sequoia High Sierra Camp:

http://www.sequoiahighsierracamp.com/

Bearpaw High Sierra Camp:

http://www.visitsequoia.com/bearpaw.aspx

5. Planning & Preparation

Given the trail's challenging profile and remote location, proper planning and preparation will be your key to successfully completing (and enjoying) the HST. The information in this chapter will help you break down the planning process into manageable stages and ensure that you'll be able to plunge into this great outdoor adventure with confidence.

a. Itinerary

The process of planning your itinerary can be broken down into two stages. The first stage includes all activities concerning long lead items, such as permits and travel arrangements. The resulting 'macro-plan' is the organizational frame of the hiking trip. The second stage focuses on determining the specifics of your hike, such as daily distances and potential campsites. The resulting 'micro-plan' is your personal hiking strategy.

Macro-Planning

The below flow chart outlines the important steps in planning the logistics of your trip. The order shown was determined based on pragmatic considerations and may be altered depending on personal preferences. Individual steps may also be omitted if not applicable.

Figure 12 – Flow Chart Macro-Planning

First, you should estimate your trail days. Be realistic about what you can achieve in terms of daily mileage and ensure that the schedule you set for yourself is right for you. The resulting duration of your hike will impact all of the subsequent macro-planning decisions. Once you know how long it will take you to hike the HST, check your calendar for times that you would be able to go. Cross-reference your schedule with those of any hiking buddies and make a list of all the date ranges that will work for your group.

Once you have this list, log on to the National Park Service website and check the availability of permits for all the date ranges identified. Fill out the permit application for each of the date ranges that work and submit it along with your deposit. If your application is processed successfully, you will receive an email within two weeks, confirming which of your requested dates were accepted. With your permit confirmation in hand and the dates locked in, you'll be ready to start booking travel and making all other necessary arrangements for your trip.

If the planning process seems like a lot of things need to happen at the same time, you'd be right. Coordinating a date range that works for you and the other members of the group (and still has available permits) is probably one of the biggest logistical challenges in planning your trip on the HST. You can help mitigate this by getting schedule commitments from your group before the permit application period opens, and then submitting your application at the earliest possible time.

Upon completion of the macro-planning step, you will have the following:

- Rough hiking schedule (starting and ending date)
- Necessary permit reserved
- Transportation plan to the trailhead at Crescent Meadow
- Transportation plan from the trailhead at Whitney Portal
- Accommodations before and after your hike (if necessary)

Micro-Planning

With your starting and ending dates decided, it's time to breakdown your time on the trail into segments that will dictate your campsite locations and daily mileage (also referred to as "trip legs" or "trail sections"). Your trip legs should be planned around not only the linear distance you expect to travel but also the elevation profile for that segment of the trip. You can expect to need more time to complete sections of the trail with significant elevation gain or loss. The easiest way to start planning your trip legs on the HST is to pick campsites for each night, taking into consideration the distance and elevation gain or loss between them, and determining whether that will work for your level of fitness and schedule or if you need to adjust. Both the overview of established HST campsites and the elevation profile of the trail provided in Appendix C are great tools to aid you in this effort.

The first step is to determine how far you will be able to travel each day. You can either estimate the distance based on your experience from previous hiking trips or calculate your average daily mileage as outlined in Section 2b *Time*, incorporating the difficulty of a particular trail section as per elevation profile. Alternatively, if you prefer a more scientific approach, you can determine your daily distance by applying Naismuth's Rule as discussed in Appendix F.

Continuing the example from Section 2b *Time*, let's assume your estimate of trail days (ETD) is 7, which results in an average daily mileage of 10.3. Using this figure, you can now look at potential campsites that fall within this range, while taking into consideration the difficulty of the respective trail section and making adjustments to the daily mileage if necessary.

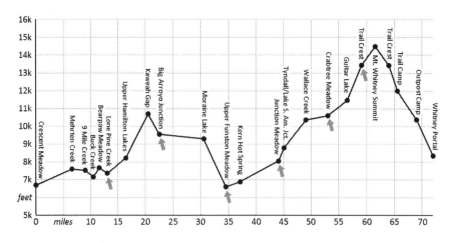

Figure 13 – Sample Trip Legs marked in Elevation Profile

In our example (see Figure 13), the distance for day 1 has been extended by a few miles (13 instead of 10), given the relatively flat terrain. In turn, the distance for day 2 has been reduced to accommodate the significant elevation gain. Once you have an idea of where you plan to camp, you can use the table below to calculate actual daily distances and elevation gains/losses.

Campsite	Distance fr. CM (miles)	Elevation (feet)	Day	Distance (miles)
Crescent Meadow (CM)	0.0	6,706		
Mehrten Creek	6.5	7,635		
9 Mile Creek	9.0	7,546		
Buck Creek	10.5	7,200		
Bearpaw Meadow	11.5	7,664		
Lone Pine Creek	13.0	7,395	1	13.0
Upper Hamilton Lakes	16.5	8,238		
Big Arroyo Junction	22.5	9,564	2	9.5
Moraine Lake	30.5	9,304		
Upper Funston Meadow	34.5	6,650	3	12.0
Kern Hot Spring	37.0	6,916		
Junction Meadow	44.0	8,074	4	9.5
Tyndall/Lake S. Am. Jct.	45.0	8,822		
Wallace Creek	49.0	10,394		
Crabtree Meadow	53.0	10,636	5	9.0
Guitar Lake	56.5	11,496		
Trail Crest (West-Side)	61.5	13,438	6	8.5
Trail Camp	65.5	12,008		
Outpost Camp	69.0	10,358		
Whitney Portal	72.0	8,373	7	10.5

Table 13 – Sample Trip Legs marked in Campsite Table

(i) In addition to your primary schedule, create a slower "Plan B" schedule of alternate trip legs and campsites. This will allow you to adjust your schedule while you're on the trail if you find that your original schedule was too aggressive or too optimistic.

Once you have created Plan A and Plan B schedules that you are happy with, mark each campsite on your topographic map along with the distance and elevation gain/loss from the previous point. This will provide you with a quick reference guide that you can check at any time during your hike to gauge how challenging the trail will be before you reach your next campsite and, if necessary, use to decide if you need to change to Plan B.

For example, if you plan on camping at Lone Pine Creek for your first night, you would mark the location on your topographic map, write "+689 ft." (approximate elevation gain from Crescent Meadow) and "13 miles" (approximate distance from Crescent Meadow).

b. Food

Your Last Meal

Next to the Lodgepole Visitors Center (where you'll pick up your permit) is the *Lodgepole Market Center*[8] which has a deli, restaurant, and general store. Here you can buy small trinkets and souvenirs for Sequoia National Park and grab a nice meal. I ate a big lunch to give me as much energy as possible before I set out on the trail. If you need something to look forward to, the Whitney Portal Store at the Mt. Whitney trailhead serves pancakes and burgers.

Food on the Trail

There are no resupply points along the route of the HST. From the time you leave Crescent Meadow, you will need to be carrying all the food necessary to cover the entire 72 miles to Whitney Portal.

Although there will be bear boxes at most of the campsites along the trail, you will need to have a bear canister for the Whitney Zone[9] at the very least. Certain side trips may also require a bear canister. In addition to keeping all your tasty food safe from all the furry animals that will want a

---

[8] Website: *http://www.visitsequoia.com/lodgepole-market-center.aspx*
[9] Map: *https://fs.usda.gov/Internet/FSE_MEDIA/stelprdb5347548.jpg*

taste, the bear canister will also serve to limit the total volume of food you can take with you, since it can only fit so much. Bear canisters come in a variety of styles and sizes, which will be further discussed in Section 6d *Food & Water*.

Trail meals can be a tricky thing to master. On the one hand, you're going to want meals that are easy and quick to prepare. On the other hand, you'll want enough variety to give you something to look forward to. If you pour eight pounds of power bars into your bear canister and hit the road, chances are good that somewhere around day four or five you may, in a moment of desperation, assault some innocent passerby and take whatever food they have that isn't bar-shaped. At the same time, you also don't want to pack like you're about to be a contestant on a Gordon Ramsey cooking show.

In between these two extremes of mono-food and impractical complexity is a magic zone where you can have food with a bit of variety that is also lightweight, easy to prepare, requires minimal clean up, and provides sufficient nourishment. Refer to Appendix B for a comprehensive list of food suggestions. Here are some guidelines that put you on the right track for picking food that will meet your needs:

- Weight: your food should be as dry and light as possible (including packaging).
- Nutritional value: combine foods to ensure an adequate supply of vitamins and minerals.
- Calorie distribution: balance approx. 15% protein, 60% carbohydrates, and 25% fat per meal.
- Non-perishable: your food must not spoil for the duration of your trip at up to 90°F (30°C).
- Easy preparation: to save stove fuel, time, dirty pots, and nerves after a long day of hiking.

Figure 14 – Food Bagged and Ready to be Packed

There are two primary components in determining how much food to bring. First, the number of calories. On average, a man will consume around 2,500 calories per day and a woman will consume around 2,000 calories per day. Your meals should provide approx. 1.5-2 times the calories you usually consume per day. Second, the amount of space it requires. Since you will need to use a bear canister, the canister you choose will dictate the maximum amount of space you have to work with. The largest single canisters store approx. 3 gallon (12l). This should be enough space to get you through about seven days if you are packing efficiently. Here are some tips for packing your bear canister:

- Remove or trim off any excess food packaging that you don't need.
- Poke a small hole in meal pouches and snack packaging to let out any excess air.
- Crush chips, crackers, and other "bulky" food items to save additional space.
- Prepackage all meals in separate resealable plastic bags and number bags based on planned day of consumption.
- Plan to consume big/heavy/perishable items before small/light/non-perishable items.

- Pack your food in reverse order of consumption (last in, first out) and create a separate layer for each day
- Food for day 1 does not need to fit in the canister since it will be eaten before going to sleep (any trash or leftovers will have to fit in the canister however)

In addition to your main meals, well-chosen snacks and supplements provide valuable nourishment. As temperatures rise, it is vital to replenish electrolytes, such as sodium, chloride, potassium, magnesium, manganese, and calcium, on a consistent basis. High water intake without electrolyte replacement over many hours can lead to hyponatremia, a life-threatening condition where your body does not have enough salts to function. Adding salty snacks (pretzels, salted nuts, chips, or electrolyte drink mixes) and/or supplements to your trail diet helps avoid electrolyte imbalance.

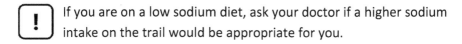 If you are on a low sodium diet, ask your doctor if a higher sodium intake on the trail would be appropriate for you.

Other Food Considerations

As you plan your meals, mind the respective cooking times and utensils needed for preparation. Anything that requires boiling or simmering for several minutes can be bothersome. Similarly, at-camp preparations, such as cutting/peeling/mashing, or meals that require a lot of attention and flipping with spatulas can be a hassle after a long day of hiking. Many hikers plan their meals so that the only cooking gear required is a small gas stove, one pot, and one spoon. Nevertheless, whatever meals you decide to go with, bring along adequate equipment and a healthy supply of patience.

After preparing food, do dishes at least 100 feet (30m) from your campsite. Likewise, be sure to pack any leftovers and store your bear canister at least 100 feet (30m) away, preferably in a shaded spot downwind of camp or in a permanent bear box (where available). Never store the bear canister or other scented items in your tent!

Another option is to skip preparing meals altogether. The author of *Plan & Go: The John Muir Trail* met a 64-year-old man on the JMT who ate nothing but power bars over the entire course of his trek and was quite content with his decision. Others eat a quick cereal bar while packing up to save time and gas for a hot breakfast later in the day. Some hikers alternate their food strategy depending on the campsite, the arrival time, and the difficulty of the day ahead. Nice spots and slow days may invite you to enjoy an extensive morning coffee or to spend a long evening with more elaborate dining. Whatever your strategy, focus on something that meets your needs with the least amount of weight and hassle.

c. Training

The HST may be among the most challenging hikes you have ever attempted, demanding more from you physically and mentally than any of your previous adventures. But fear not, with appropriate training, a solid foundation of physical fitness, and some mental fortitude, you will make it across the finish line.

Mental Preparation

The right attitude in every phase of a long-distance hike is just as important as proper physical and logistical preparation. From the moment you make the decision, through the weeks of planning your trip, to the final day on the trail, maintaining an open mind and a resilient attitude in coping with obstacles is essential. At any given point, you may be confronted with fatigue, anxiety, or doubt. In those moments, remind yourself that even the smallest steps in the right direction will help you eventually achieve the goal.

Physical Preparation

Endurance and strength are indispensable assets when it comes to going the full distance of a long hike. If your body is not used to walking long distances for multiple days in a row while carrying up to 45lbs of extra weight, you are going to need some conditioning. Individual workout needs may vary based on age, health, current fitness level, and other factors. Ultimately, the most important thing is to get your body used to a high level of physical activity. To avoid injury, start slow and gradually increase the intensity.

A good training routine will incorporate cardiovascular exercises and weight lifting elements. Go hiking frequently and participate in other forms of aerobic fitness like cycling, swimming, running, or group fitness classes. This will not only increase your endurance, but also build confidence and momentum for your adventure. Exercise with light to medium weights to strengthen shoulder and back muscles.

A good training exercise is the "90-degree lateral dumbbell raise". Stand with your feet at shoulder's width, your back slightly slanted forward, and your core muscles engaged. Start by holding the weights in your hands with your elbows at a 90-degree angle touching your ribs and your forearms extended straight in front of your body. In a slow, smooth motion, raise elbows from your ribs to shoulder's height. Hold briefly and return to the starting position.

(i) Choose a weight that allows you to do at least three sets of 15-20 repetitions and remember to engage both your abdominal as well as your lower back muscles to support a sturdy stance.

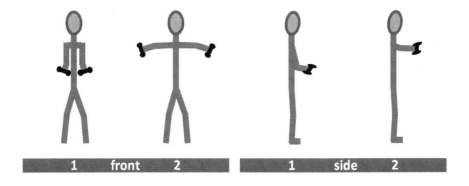

Figure 15 – 90 Degree Dumbbell Lateral Raise

As your fitness level improves, it is crucial to add weight to some of your cardio exercises to simulate the backpack you will be carrying on the trail.

Begin by wearing an empty pack, then a partially weighted pack, and eventually the equivalent weight of what you plan to carry during the trip. Progress to steeper terrain to increase the difficulty and diversity your training regimen.

> **!** The areas of your body most heavily stressed during the hike are your feet, shins, knees, back, and hips. If you've had problems with any of these parts historically, it will be particularly important to do some long training hikes to gauge and prepare for how your body will respond to the conditions on the HST.

Hiking Style

A good hiking style will help you use your energy efficiently and minimize the strain on your joints and tendons. This includes hiking at a sustainable pace, taking small controlled steps, and placing your feet in the direction of the slope.

Hike at a Sustainable Pace

The HST is an ultra-marathon, not a sprint. From an athletic perspective, this means that you need to keep your metabolism and energy conversion in an aerobic state. In brief, aerobic metabolism means that your muscles are receiving enough oxygen from your lungs, sufficient fuel through your bloodstream, and have enough time to dispose of by-products from burning the fuel, especially lactic acid.

The aerobic state of respiration is usually the sweet spot for your body to process its energy from both a nutritional intake and a body fat perspective. Keep in mind that even very fit people have an average body fat level of 5-15 percent. That means that a 160lbs person could have around 16lbs of fat which contains approx. 56,000 calories – enough caloric energy for over 20 days. Tapping into this body fat on the trail will help keep your packed food weight low and have the happy side effect of helping you shed a couple of pounds during the trip.

Your personal sustainable pace will vary depending on your level of fitness, the altitude, trail conditions, and the temperature, among other factors. Finding your personal sustainable pace is simple. It is the pace at which you breathe deeply, but not rushed. You may sweat, but never excessively. You feel you could hike like this for hours without having to stop frequently. A slow but sustainable pace will ultimately be the fastest because you will be less fatigued and need less rest/recovery time.

Take Small Steps

Small steps can help reduce both the force of impact on your joints and the likelihood of a misstep or injury. You will be climbing and descending tall rock or dirt steps on many parts of the trail. Rather than leaping or taking a large step, you can use 2-3 well-placed steps to reduce the effort you would need to expend on a single ambitious move. This will minimize the strain on your muscles, reducing exhaustion, and extend the distance you will be able to travel that day.

Descending with a full pack can result in knee, ankle, and shin pain. The larger the step, the greater the vertical drop and the greater the impact on your joints. Small steps are also less likely to go wrong as they have less momentum that could potentially cause you to twist your ankle or slip on loose gravel or other slippery surfaces.

Always Place Your Feet in the Direction of the Slope

This recommendation is especially important when hiking downhill. Look at the direction and angle of the slope. Always place your foot so that it is in line with the direction of the slope of the trail. If the path is going straight down the mountain, your toes should also point straight down.

Why? Think of it this way: if you do slip, you want your toes to shoot forward so that you fall backwards. You may land on your bottom or your backpack, but both are padded. If you had your foot sideways and slipped, you could roll your ankle or land hard on your side.

Trekking Poles

Various forums and literature state that the proper use of trekking poles may increase your daily distance by up to 25%. Regardless of whether or not this is accurate for you, trekking poles do provide definite advantages when used correctly. Here are some of the highlights:

- Increased stability in crossing streams on rocks/logs or wading.
- Increased stability while descending in mud/sand/loose gravel.
- Increased forward thrust and momentum.
- Reduced leg fatigue by recruiting upper body muscles.
- Reduced impact on legs/joints when descending slopes or steps.
- More effective rest while standing.
- Wave overhead and bang together to scare off animals.
- Probe ahead of you to discover snakes when trail is overgrown.
- Probe depth of water and firmness of snow.

Using hiking poles correctly is essential to unlocking their potential. Most poles will be adjustable in length, although some of the lower-end models as well as some ultralight models may be fixed-length. I recommend that you use adjustable-length poles as they have the additional benefit of being able to collapse down to a size that will make storing them easier when they are not in use.

Poles should be adjusted so that when standing still with the pole held upright, your arm is bent at a roughly 90° angle. Lock down or twist the poles to securely hold the length in place. Lean on the poles to test them – they shouldn't begin to slowly collapse down under your weight. Put your hands through the straps and then grasp the handle so that if you let go of the handle, the strap will act like a bracelet and keep the pole dangling from your arm. Adjust the straps so that they fit comfortably around your wrists and your hands can grip the handles loosely. Only when you lift the pole from its rearmost position, firm your grip with pinky and ring finger to elevate the pole's tip from the ground.

For thrust to propel yourself forward, keep the tips of poles behind you as shown in Figure 16 below. In this position, smoothly but forcefully push back with one arm at a time as you stride forward. Swing your arms in a natural and comfortable fashion, planting then pushing off with the poles as you do so. Engage and repeat.

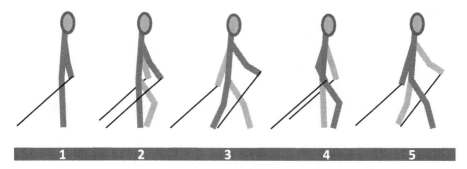

Figure 16 – Trekking Pole Use

Be sure not to ram the poles into the ground. This causes stress on your wrists and shoulders and leads to earlier exhaustion. When traveling on flat sections of the trail, you will want your energy to go into forward movement, not straight into the ground. Note how in Figure 16 the poles are never vertical but always at an angle, so that you push forward and not down. If you do decide to use trekking poles on the HST (which I recommend), make sure to familiarize yourself with the right technique before you go. There are plenty of video tutorials out there which can be helpful in this regard.

(i) If you're new to using hiking poles, it would be wise to try them out on a few hikes to see how they feel and to get in a bit of practice before you hit the HST.

6. Gear

Figure 17 – Some of my Gear on the Trail

Gear selection could easily be a separate book in itself. It is outside of the scope of this book to try and provide an exhaustive list of different types of gear and the pros and cons for various gear selection strategies. The following overview is intended to introduce the most commonly used items and provide HST-specific recommendations to aid your decision-making. In addition, I highly recommend you visit your local outdoor outfitter and do some additional research online to further evaluate different alternatives.

a. Clothing

You will be faced with a wide variety of temperatures on the HST, ranging from the very hot to the very cold. Choosing efficient clothing will be essential to keep your weight down while enabling you to respond to the temperatures you will encounter. Regardless of the weather forecast, don't venture out onto the HST without appropriate attire to deal with rain and temperatures below freezing.

Layering

Since you will not have the luxury of taking a closet full of clothes on the HST, you will need to take advantage of a clothing strategy known as "layering." Layering is the concept of wearing multiple layers of clothes which you can add to or subtract from in order to provide you with more or less warmth and protection. The first layer against your skin is called the *base layer*. The base layer helps control your body temperature by moving perspiration away from your skin, so fabrics with excellent moisture-wicking capabilities are highly preferable. The next layer, called *middle layer*, provides insulation to help retain heat by trapping air close to your body. The outer layer, called the *shell layer*, provides protection from the elements. For additional warmth and comfort during extra cold conditions, consider taking a set of thermal underwear top and bottom.

Below are a few sample clothing combinations based on the weather situations you are likely to encounter. The gear is listed in the order in which you put it on. For instance, in cold weather, you will wear your thermal layer, then your hiking shirt, then your jacket, and then your jacket shell.

Hot or Warm Weather Outfit

- Top: hiking shirt
- Bottom: underwear, convertible pants
- Feet: sock liners, socks
- Hands: none
- Head: wide-brimmed hat

Cool Weather Outfit

- Top: hiking shirt, jacket or jacket shell
- Bottom: underwear, convertible pants
- Feet: sock liners, socks
- Hands: gloves
- Head: beanie or wide-brimmed hat

Cold Weather Outfit

- Top: thermal layer, hiking shirt, jacket, jacket shell
- Bottom: underwear, thermal layer, convertible pants, pants shell
- Feet: sock liners, socks
- Hands: glove liners, gloves
- Head: multifunctional scarf, beanie, jacket shell hood

Rain Outfit

- Top: hiking shirt, jacket shell
- Bottom: underwear, convertible pants, pants shell
- Feet: sock liners, socks
- Hands: gloves
- Head: multifunctional scarf, wide-brimmed hat

Unless I was extremely cold, I tended to start my days with my hiking shirt, hiking pants, jacket, and beanie. I could then shed my jacket and beanie quickly and easily as my body temperature and the air temperature started to heat up. Given the total lack of shade at higher elevations and regular exposure to the sun during most of your trip, a long sleeve shirt, pants, a wide brimmed hat, sunglasses, and sunblock should all be employed simultaneously to give you the highest level of sun protection possible.

Clothing Options

Shorts vs. Pants

Fortunately, you don't really have to choose between shorts and pants. Thanks to the miracle of modern technology, you can have both in a single pair of trousers. These convertible pants have zippers at the knees, enabling you to zip off the bottom section and turn those pants into shorts. It is the only pair of pants I ever take with me. When choosing a pair, make sure that the back of the zipper (the part that will be inside your pant leg) is covered by a flap of fabric so that the zipper doesn't rub against your skin. If you have to go with either shorts or pants, go with pants. They will keep you cleaner, warmer, and offer you greater protection against the sun. The most notable drawback being that you'll be hot on certain sections of the trail.

Short Sleeve vs. Long Sleeve Shirt

Hiking shirts come in a wide variety of styles and qualities. Generally speaking, they are lightweight, quick-drying, have a collar that can be turned up to protect your neck from the sun, and provide UV protection. As with convertible hiking pants, there are shirts which bring the best of both long sleeve and short sleeve into a single, convenient package. More advanced hiking shirts have multiple pockets, sleeves which can be rolled up and buttoned in place (making them short-sleeved), and vents in various places to help you stay cool even in hot temperatures.

Down vs. Synthetic

You will need a good warm jacket for the HST. The major choice you will have to make in choosing a jacket is whether to go synthetic or down. Generally speaking, down is thought to be warmer and lighter but loses its insulating properties if it gets wet, while synthetic is better when wet but a bit heavier and not quite as warm. Synthetics seem to be making ground on closing the warmth-gap between the two with each passing year, and it would be reasonable to consider that the two are pretty equivalent at this point. I personally went with a synthetic jacket in case it accidentally got wet from a fall into a river, lake, etc.

Avoid Cotton!

Under no circumstances should any article of clothing you take with you on the HST be made of cotton. Cotton rapidly absorbs moisture, takes a long time to dry, and loses its ability to keep you warm when it gets wet. In hiking circles, cotton is often referred to as the "fabric of death." Clothing specifically designed for hiking and made from various synthetic materials or wool (e.g., merino wool) is a much better option for you on any long-distance hike.

Additional Clothing

Rain Gear

You will need a good rain jacket/wind breaker (also referred to as a "jacket shell" since it typically has little to no insulation of its own and goes over your insulating jacket). This jacket will be rain- and windproof and will help you stay dry and warm in the harshest conditions you will encounter on the trail. Keep in mind that you will need to get a shell large enough to wear over your warm jacket. Buy a shell that is a size larger than you think you'll need if you're purchasing online or try it on over a jacket if you are buying in a store. The same applies to the "pants shell".

Head Gear

You'll need two pieces of headgear. One for cold temperatures and one for sun protection. For cold, consider a jacket with a built-in hood plus some additional head protection (e.g., beanie, multifunctional scarf, balaclava). A hooded jacket will give you one less article of gear to keep track of, and since it will be sown to your jacket, it will keep your neck warmer than a jacket and hat combination. You also never need to worry that it will be blown off a mountainside in the wind. For protecting your face and neck from relentless high-elevation sun, consider taking a wide-brimmed hat.

Sleeping

Depending on the temperature outside, the type of shelter you have, how hot your body temperature tends to run, and the thermal rating of your sleeping bag, you either may want to wear multiple layers of clothing or nothing at all inside your sleeping bag. Your thermal layers are great for sleep wear as they tend to be warm but not bulky. Since you'll be wearing them only during the coldest times on the trail, they are less likely to be covered in sweat and trail dust (unlike your other clothes).

At Camp

Flip-flops or other very lightweight sandals can be a useful addition to your packing list. These can be used after arriving at camp and before you bed down for the night – giving the inside of your shoes a bit more time to dry and your feet a welcome bit of fresh air before you stuff them into the bottom of your sleeping bag.

Example Clothing List

Below is a list of all of the clothing I took on the HST:

1 Long sleeve hiking shirt	1 Thermal/long underwear bottom
1 Convertible hiking pants	1 Thermal/long underwear top
3 Socks	1 Synthetic down jacket
2 Sock liners	1 Beanie
2 Underwear	1 Multifunctional scarf
1 Wide-brimmed hat	1 Gloves
1 Trail shoes	1 Glove liners
1 Belt	1 Jacket shell
1 Sunglasses	1 Pants shell

b. Hiking

In addition to clothing, basic hiking gear usually consists of appropriate footwear, a fitting and well-balanced backpack, and optional trekking poles. This section provides an overview of available options and features, discusses pros and cons, and offers advice on how to carefully choose and properly fit individual items.

Shoes & Boots

Having a well-fitting pair of boots or shoes will be essential on the HST. Suitable models will have thick cushioning soles with non-slip tread. Additional criteria are ankle support and protection, water resistance, breathability, weight, and overall fit and comfort. There are three typical styles – hiking boot, hiking shoe, and trail runner – that each have their individual benefits and drawbacks as outlined below.

Hiking Boots provide more stability overall. A well-fitting boot is snug, supports the ankle and reduces the risk of twisting on a slight misstep. With more contact area, the foot is less likely to move back and forth in a good boot. The high rising sides also offer ankle protection from hitting rocks and prevent sand and dust from entering the boot. Other advantages are warmth and water resistance, however, neither are particularly necessary for the HST. Drawbacks of boots are the greater weight, stiffness, and lower breathability.

| Hiking Boot | Hiking Shoe | Trail Runner |

Figure 18 – Hiking Shoes & Boots[10]

Hiking Shoes combine the grip stability of a good boot with more flexibility. The low cut allows more mobility and light mesh uppers enable moisture wicking. Look for a pair with firm heel support and a plastic or rubber tip to protect your toes. Different brands have various lacing systems, some enable great fit in minimal time. Hiking shoes are lighter than boots and generally feel less restrictive while still providing sufficiently firm stability. Drawbacks are potentially more rocks and sand in your shoes, reduced ankle support, and reduced ankle protection.

Trail Runners go even further in the agility and lightweight categories, weighing about as much as a conventional running shoe. In order to save weight, trail runners usually provide less cushioning than hiking shoes,

---

[10] Sketches of Asolo boot and Salomon shoes

while still offering good tread and lots of grip. Upper materials are mostly breathable, light meshes, offering more support than running shoes but far less than a boot. Quick lacing systems are also available. Trail runners are appropriate for a run in the mountains or woods, not necessarily for long hiking trips with heavy backpacks. They have low overall support and cushioning. I would not recommend taking them on the HST.

I personally prefer hiking shoes over boots for the HST since they weigh less, breathe better, and still maintain good cushioning, grip, and support. Consider opting for boots if you plan on going for any significant off-trail adventures as the additional ankle support will be helpful once you're off the well-worn path. The shoe does not have to be especially water resistant, as rain, wet crossings, and snow should not be an issue most of the time. I would not recommend trail running shoes as they are not designed to support long hikes with heavy gear on your back.

If at all possible, I recommend going to a reputable outdoor outfitter to get fitted for your hiking boots/shoes. If you order online, get them at least half a size bigger than you normally would. Do not settle for anything that isn't *incredibly* comfortable. Your hiking shoes should provide your toes with enough room to not brush the front of the inside when trudging downhill, yet not so much room that your foot slides around inside since that can lead to blisters. They need to be snug, but not tight. They need to fit comfortably when you are wearing the exact pairs of hiking socks and sock liners that you intend to wear on your trip.

No matter how comfortable they are in the store, you are not done picking your shoes until you have tested them outside. Take them for a few test hikes in conditions that are similar to the HST. Long duration (10+ mile single-session hikes) with both uphill and downhill slopes while carrying a fully-loaded backpack will give you an idea of what they will feel like when you put them to the test and will also help break them in. If you hit the trail with a pair of shoes that you just pulled out of the box for the first time, you're going to regret it.

Socks & Gaiters

A good sock can significantly add to your hiking comfort. Most modern trail socks are made of merino wool or polyester. Both fibers have outstanding properties regarding moisture wicking and temperature regulation. Thick socks, especially those with hidden seams, provide cushioning and help the shoe embrace your foot evenly, reducing rubbing and blisters. Though less stylish in a shoes-shorts combo and slightly warmer, socks that go (well) above your ankle collect less sand and stones, keep your legs cleaner, and provide better protection from the sun.

Gaiters can provide even greater protection for your feet and lower legs. They wrap around your ankles and calves and cover the gap between socks and footwear. There are different types of gaiters to choose from depending on the nature of the trip and the conditions expected. Low-rise trail gaiters are perfect for the HST. They are lightweight, breathable, and provide basic protection against rocks, grit, and snow.

Compression socks can assist circulation and provide additional benefits to those who have issues with blood clots, edema, and thrombosis. They come in different lengths, from knee- and thigh-high, to full pantyhose style, and in a variety of compression gradients. Lower gradients are usually prescription free while higher gradients may require consultation. If you are over 40 years old or have a condition where they could be helpful, consult with a doctor to determine your options.

Backpack

Just like shoes, an ill-fitting backpack can be a source of considerable pain. Chaffing along straps, restrictive harnesses, poorly adjusted hip belts, and other issues can quickly impact both your speed and enjoyment on the trail.

Choosing a Pack

There is a wide variety of pack sizes, styles, and brands to choose from. Below are some criteria that will help you find the pack that is right for you. In addition to this information, consider reading online product reviews of various makes and models to see how other hikers have rated the pack's performance. If possible, get fitted for your pack by a professional at a reputable outdoor outfitter. Take a fully loaded pack on training hikes before the HST to make sure it still feels good after long hikes with substantial weight.

Criteria	Comment
Size	<table><tr><td>Size</td><td>Torso [in.]</td><td>Torso [cm]</td></tr><tr><td>Extra Small</td><td>up to 15 ½</td><td>up to 40</td></tr><tr><td>Small</td><td>15 ½ - 17½</td><td>40 - 45</td></tr><tr><td>Medium</td><td>17½ - 19½</td><td>45 - 50</td></tr><tr><td>Large</td><td>19½ and up</td><td>50 and up</td></tr></table> These are commonly used sizes. Information on how to measure your torso is provided later in this section. In addition to the torso height, the design and cut of packs and shoulder straps vary to make them more comfortable for broad or narrow shouldered people. Compare and try different packs.
Capacity	Packing capacity is measured in liters. A pack with a capacity of 65-80 liters should suffice to accommodate all the gear you will take with you on the HST. While you shouldn't take a pack larger than you need, you want to make sure it has enough capacity to easily fit your gear. Having a little extra room will make it much easier to pack and repack your gear throughout the trip, which will ultimately save you a lot of time and headaches. The pack capacity you need generally depends on the spatial requirements for your bulkiest items (tent, sleeping bag, sleeping pad, bear canister) and how much space your clothing will take. Packs allow some

	flexibility by raising the top lid or strapping a tent or foam pad to the outside. However, this may mean that weights are not optimally distributed. See the *Packing & Adjusting Your Pack* sections further below for additional information.
Weight	As with most other gear, the weight of a backpack is closely linked to comfort and price. Thick, comfortable padding along shoulder straps and hip belts add weight. However, keep in mind that you will be carrying this pack all day for an extended period of time, so increasing the weight by adding additional comfort may be worthwhile. The durability of materials also affects the pack's weight. Light packs usually have thinner shell materials. Tearing and punctures could be a problem if you aren't careful where and how you set your pack down. Lighter packs may also be less water resistant, but since significant rain on the HST is unlikely, you probably don't need to consider this feature in your decision.
Padding	You will be carrying this heavy pack for hours at a time, several days in a row. The padding and structure of the shoulder straps, hip belt, and where the frame touches your back are essential to how comfortable your pack will be especially when filled with up to 45lbs (20kg) of gear. Ultralight packs typically cut out some of the padding and pack structure to save weight. These types of packs are best for people with a full kit of ultralight gear. Loading up an ultralight pack with heavy gear is going to make your hike uncomfortable.
Adjustability	Most modern internal frame packs are very similar regarding their adjustability. Shoulder straps and hip belts can be adjusted in length; load lifter straps connect the pack's top to the shoulder straps and keep the weight balanced near your center; sternum straps connect the shoulder straps across the chest to snug

	the pack's fit and increase stability. Some packs have an adjustable suspension system, meaning the entire shoulder harness system can be slid up and down to customize the pack to the exact torso length. Compression straps along the sides and front of the pack pull the weight close to your center and keep contents from shifting on difficult trails. Daisy chains[11], elastic straps, trekking pole loops, and other tool loops allow you to arrange and adjust gear on the outside of the pack.
Compartments	A pack with a well thought-out design can make your life a lot easier on the trail. Most packs come with a plethora of pouches, compartments, straps, and other storage amenities. The right combination of compartments is largely a matter of personal preference. Some hikers may insist on a sleeping bag compartment at the bottom of the pack, others may look for a minimum number of side pockets to organize and access the contents of their pack, while still others may want one or two water bottle pockets.
Ventilation	A well-ventilated back area can be a big plus, especially on the hottest sections of the trail. A dry back and shoulders not only add to your general comfort but make your body less susceptible to chaffing. Different brands and models have various approaches for wicking moisture and heat from in-between your back and your pack. Some have air channels between padding, others completely separate the pack from the hiker's back with a tension mesh. Some ventilation methods are more effective and/or comfortable than others. Try them out until you find one that you like.
Hydration	A standard feature on most packs and one which is worth asking about is a place inside the pack to store

---

[11] Daisy chain: A series of vertical loops of webbing, usually placed up along the center of the pack on the outside.

	a water bladder. These packs will have a small slit for the drinking tube and elastic rings or clips on the shoulder straps that allow you to attach the tube for convenient access.
Frame	There are two frame styles: internal and external frames. Almost all modern packs are internal frame and have the frame sewn directly into the pack. External frame packs usually have large aluminum tubes extending above and around the pack. Advantages of the external frame packs are low cost, light weight, and easy packability of bulky items (esp. on the outside). Disadvantages are their limited adjustability and fit, they are less stable on uneven terrain, and they are usually less water resistant. Internal packs make up for the above disadvantages, but are usually more expensive and heavier.
Rain cover	A built-in rain cover, usually located in the top lid or at the bottom of the pack, can be wrapped around the entire backpack with an elastic trimming. They are very practical, but not crucial on the HST. If your pack does not have a built-in rain cover, you can purchase a lightweight one that will fit your pack or improvise with a waterproof piece of material.

Table 14 – Backpack Decision Criteria

Convenient access to my gear, pockets to separate and organize everything, external straps for lightweight gear, and a comfortable suspension and padding system are high priorities for me in choosing a pack. For multi-day backpacking trips, I personally like packs that have several exterior pockets, daisy chains, and straps that can be used to tie gear to the outside, loops to stow hiking-poles, water bladder features, a separate sleeping bag section at the bottom of the pack, a mesh-vented section where the pack rests against my back, both top and side-loading capabilities, and moderate to heavy shoulder and hip padding.

The best and easiest way to choose a pack size is to visit a well-regarded outdoor outfitter and have one of their experts fit you for a pack. This will give you an opportunity to try a variety of packs with different features, weights, and price ranges. Ask them if they can load the pack up with some weight and walk around the store with it so you can get a feel for what it will be like when it's full of gear. If going to a store is not an option, or if you want to buy a pack online, you can use the following approach:

Side Note – Measuring your torso length:

1. Locate your 7th cervical vertebra (C7) at the base of your neck by tilting your head forward. It is the bony bump at the end your vertical spine as your neck is leaning forward. When you run your fingers down your neck, you will first feel the smaller C6 and then C7. This marks the top of your torso.

2. Locate your iliac crest at the top of your hip bone by placing your hands high on your hips. With your thumbs in the back, dig into your pelvis to find the rounded, highest point of your hip bone. The imaginary line between your thumbs marks the bottom of your torso.

3. Measure between top and bottom of your torso. Be sure to stand straight and have a friend measure the distance between the top and bottom of your torso. Assistance while handling the tape measure is helpful.

Packing your Pack

As you pack your backpack, pay attention to two things: the weight distribution and the internal organization of your gear.

Regarding *weight distribution*, it is important to keep heavy items close to your back and centered both vertically and horizontally (see Figure 19). Moderately heavy items should be placed closest to the heavy items, leaving the perimeter of the pack (sleeping bag compartment, exterior straps) for the lightest weight items. The aim is to bring the weight in the backpack as close to the center of your back as possible. This way, the pack's center of gravity is closest to your own, making it less likely for you to lose your balance and reducing the strain on your back.

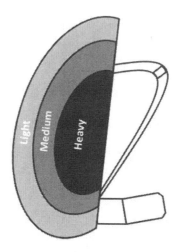

Figure 19 – Backpack Weight Distribution

A well-planned *internal organization* and distribution of gear among the compartments and pockets of your pack can save time and headaches. Anything that needs easy and frequent access, such as a map, sunscreen, snacks, or a pocket knife, should be stored in an accessible outside pocket near/on the top of your pack. Gear that will only be used once at camp can be placed inside and below heavy items. How exactly you pack your backpack will be dictated largely by the total pack capacity, pack features like compartments or straps, and the size and shape of your gear. Pack and unpack your gear at home and during your training hikes to determine best packing order and location of various pieces of gear. Sticking to a particular gear organization structure and routine will make it easier to pack your backpack and access crucial gear while on the go.

Using thin plastic bags or (water-resistant) compression sacks can be a good way to further organize your pack's main compartment. You can use these to group certain types of gear (cooking set, sleep clothes, etc.) and make accessing contents more convenient while providing additional protection against water and dirt. Valuables (phone, keys, money) can be kept in a zip lock bag and buried, as they will hardly be needed. Keep rain gear easily accessible, so you can get it out quickly in a thunderstorm. Once you have all your items packed and are ready to hit the trail, pull all the compression straps (usually on the sides and top of your pack) to bring the weight closer to your back and prevent gear from shifting during the hike.

Adjusting your Pack

Step 1: Adjusting your pack starts by putting it on correctly. If your pack is heavy, place one foot forward and lift the pack onto your thigh, a nearby rock or other surface at a convenient level. Then, slip into the shoulder straps and lean forward, pulling the pack onto your back (if you're not familiar with this technique, search for a tutorial video online). As you lean forward, position the pack so the hip belt is centered comfortably over your hip bone, then close and tighten the hip belt firmly.

Step 2: As you straighten yourself up, your shoulder straps should be loose, leaving 100% of the pack's weight on your hips. In this starting position, the shoulder straps should have a gap of approx. one inch over your shoulders. If the straps already put pressure on your shoulders in the starting position and your pack has an adjustable suspension, slide the entire shoulder harness up a little and re-secure it. Now, tighten your shoulder straps until they touch your shoulders.

Step 3: Unlike older backpack designs, today's packs use the hip belt, rather than the shoulder straps, to carry most of the pack weight. Keep this in mind as you adjust and tighten the straps. Pull your load lifters (that extend from the top of your shoulder straps to the top of your pack) to bring the pack's center of gravity closer to yours. Finally, close your sternum strap and tighten comfortably in front of your chest to help reduce the pack's tendency to pull your shoulders back. Once you have everything set, check your shoulder straps one last time to ensure that they are guiding the pack weight and keeping it close to your center of gravity, but not bearing a lot of the pack's weight.

Trekking Poles

Section 5c *Training* offered some advice on how to correctly use trekking poles and reasons why you might want to take them on the HST. Below are some features to look for when purchasing trekking poles:

- Good fitting grips and comfortable, padded wrist straps: avoid sweat-prone plastic grips (opt for cork instead) and unpadded straps that will chafe your wrists and hands.
- The length of the pole should be easily adjustable.
- The locking mechanism (twist or external lever) as well as the overall pole should be sturdy.
- The lighter the pole, the better. Lightweight poles will minimize arm fatigue and make them easier to use.
- Shock absorbers can be useful but are mostly a matter of taste. Try them out for yourself.
- Rubber tips absorb shock and muffle impact noise. More grip on rock, less on soft subsoil.
- Baskets (plastic discs just above the tip) help give you traction and additional surface area that is useful in sandy soil and snow.

c. Sleeping

This section provides an overview of the sleeping gear available to you and offers some pros and cons for the various options. For most, this will consist of a tent, sleeping bag, and sleeping pad, however, there are other alternatives to consider as well.

Shelters

When choosing a shelter, the decision comes down to how much weight you want to carry, how much money you want to spend, and how much protection you want from the elements. The pros and cons of the three most common shelter options are discussed below. If you are hiking with one or more other people, you might consider sharing a shelter to save weight. This, however, should be carefully weighed up against the benefits of having a separate shelter, which will offer a bit of privacy after a long day of hiking together.

Single-Tent   Bivy   Tarp

Figure 20 – Sleeping Shelter Options[12]

Tent

Of the three shelter options, a tent generally provides the most space and best protection from the elements for you and your gear. While the lightest single person tents are only around 1.5lbs (.7kg), carrying a tent is likely to be the heaviest option for shelter. Since most lightweight tents utilize extremely thin fabric, you will want to take a footprint (a thin sheet of tent-like material that goes under your tent) to protect the tent floor from punctures and moisture. Some tents have additional features such as a vestibule[13] or the ability to use your trekking poles instead of dedicated tent poles to reduce weight. I recommend taking a tent with a solid floor (rather than bottomless or mosquito netting floor) to reduce the chances that critters get in and bug you while sleeping.

Unlike a tarp which only gives you protection from the top and perhaps a side or two, a tent will give you thorough protection from the top, bottom, and sides. A tent also offers a bit more of a luxurious camping experience in exchange for a longer set up time and typically a bit more weight than you will find in a bivy. Unless you are very concerned with speed and

---

[12] Tent: Big Agnes, Bivy: Outdoor Research, Tarp: Kelty
[13] Vestibule: the staked-out front extension of a tent's rainfly that forms a sheltered area outside of the sleeping compartment of the tent

weight and know what you are getting into with either of the alternatives, a tent is your best option for the HST.

Bivy

A "bivy" (short for bivouac sack) is slightly bigger than a sleeping bag. The sleeping bag slides into the bivy, which is made of water and wind resistant material. A bivy bag has a small hole or breathable fabric in the head area and can be left open or zipped shut. It also has a little dome in the head area, giving some space to rest on your elbows inside. While bivies and tents offer similar insulation and protection from the elements, inner condensation is a greater problem in a bivy, because it gets in direct contact with the sleeping bag and has less air circulation. Unlike tents, bivies offer no additional room for gear or body movement. For people suffering from claustrophobia, the confined space may be problematic.

Under the Stars/Tarp

To anyone counting ounces, a tent or even bivy might sound like an unnecessary amount of weight. Light weight is in fact the only thing tarps have going for them when compared to other shelter options. They will offer you limited to no wind protection, no insulation from the cold, require trees or other tall objects to be useful, and staying dry could be a challenge in the (rather unlikely) event that you get rain at night. Unless you are already very comfortable with camping under a tarp, I would not recommend you try it on the HST. At higher elevations you might be hard-pressed to find anything to tie it to, leaving you with the world's most disappointing quilt as your only shelter.

In summary, for most hikers, the additional hassle of a tarp or a bivy will be quickly outweighed by the protection and comfort of a lightweight tent. For my trip, I took a single person tent, which utilized one of my hiking poles as the sole support in the middle, and added a footprint for some extra protection. This system worked very well at almost every campsite. The only place I found it less than ideal was when I needed to camp along the trail instead of at one of the many established campsites. It took some effort to find a flat clearing in the vegetation that was big enough for the tent itself, let alone sufficient to extend the tension cords in the directions necessary to keep the tent structure upright. As with any tent that requires stakes and tension to hold it up (as opposed to being "free-standing"), the degree of difficulty you will have pounding stakes in the ground is highly dependent on what the ground is made of. Soft, loamy soil? No problem. Granite slabs? Hope you can find some big rocks to anchor those lines to instead.

Sleeping Bags

Sleeping bags come in an overwhelming number of varieties. A good sleeping bag is a significant investment that should last for 15+ years. Because of this, try to get a sleeping bag that will work for the HST as well as other adventures you may want to take in the future. The following are some important features to consider when selecting a sleeping bag. Choosing the right bag will ultimately be a compromise between the features you want and the amount of money you are willing to spend.

Warmth

Warmth, expressed by the bag's temperature rating, will probably be the most important criteria in bag selection. Fortunately, there is an EN Standard[14] warmth measurement that lets you easily compare different bags. Choose a bag with a temperature rating equal to or lower than the average monthly low temperature for wherever you will be camping. For the HST, a three-season bag rated between 20°F - 30°F (-6°C - -1°C) should suffice for most people, but if you tend to be cold or hot when you sleep, be sure to factor that in. Keep in mind that you can always wear your clothes inside the sleeping bag if you need additional warmth.

---

[14] EN Standard 13537: a European Standard (also used by some U.S. companies) for the testing, rating, and labelling of sleeping bags.

Peak performance sleeping bags use down insulation with fill-powers[15] of 700-900 or an equivalent synthetic composition. Down is breathable and provides incredible loft and resulting insolation while being lightweight and compressing well. Additionally, there are new hydrophobic/dry downs that maintain insulation properties after getting wet and/or repel moisture. Modern synthetic fill materials mimic the great properties of down, often at a very competitive price.

Weight

Weight is an important factor in bag selection. Lower quality bags and those with more insulation (thus capable of handling lower temperatures) will generally be heavier. In an effort to reduce weight and bulk, many modern backpacking sleeping bags do not have padding on the side you will be lying on. There are two main reasons for this. First, the bag makers assume that most people will use a sleeping pad, which provides cushioning and insulation. Second, lying on the bag insulation compresses it and significantly reduces its effectiveness. Down-fill mummy bags will generally have the best warmth-to-weight ratios.

Cut and Features

Cut refers to the bag's shape. Most backpacking bags are mummy style and follow the contours of the body – wider at the shoulders and narrower along legs and feet. Some bags offer more leg room than mummy bags but consequently have more material for you to carry. Sleeping bag features include hoods, draft tubes[16], pillow cases, pockets to slide in your sleeping pad, and inside pockets to hold small items. Ultimately, you need to be comfortable when you're sleeping. The materials should feel pleasant, and you should have sufficient space around your shoulders, hips, and feet.

---

[15] Fill-power: a measure of loft in cubic inches; it describes to what volume one ounce of down expands to.

[16] Draft tube: an insulating flap or tube that covers the zipper to avoid heat loss out of the sleeping bag.

Some may find mummy sleeping bags to be confining while others like the snug feeling.

Pack Size

The amount of pack space a sleeping bag takes up is strongly correlated with the bag's temperature rating, weight, and cost. Reducing the bag weight usually reduces the pack size, and more expensive bags will typically pack down to a smaller size. Warmer bags with more filling typically do not compress as much and will take more pack space.

Shelter Compatibility

Lastly, your choice of sleeping bag should match your choice of shelter. If you are sleeping with only a tarp or completely without a shelter, your sleeping bag should be especially warm, wind and water resistant. Keep in mind that water-resistant shells are less breathable and require more time for your bag to loft. If you are planning to save weight on filling by wearing your jacket to sleep, make sure the sleeping bag provides enough inner space for the jacket's loft.

In my experience, bag temperature ratings can be rather inaccurate and generally overstate the point at which I would be still cozy and comfortable if the outside temperature drops that low. I compensate by either buying bags with a temperature rating 10-15 degrees lower than what I think I will need, by using a sleeping bag liner, or by wearing additional clothes to bed. The latter being the cheapest and lightest option.

In general, I'm not a fan of mummy bags as I am most comfortable sleeping on my stomach with one leg bent, a maneuver which is virtually impossible in the confined space of a mummy bag. The price for my extra legroom is a bit less warmth and probably a little more material to carry around.

Sleeping Pads

Sleeping pads go underneath your sleeping bag and provide cushioning and insulation. You can count on the ground being hard and cold wherever you camp along the HST. There are three popular and equally suitable types of sleeping pad:

Air Pads – Similar to the ones used in swimming pools, hiking air pads have a thin air-tight shell that is inflated through a mouth valve. In order to cut down on weight, they are often semi-rectangular in shape. Air pads are generally very lightweight, roll up very small, and offer exceptional cushioning, especially those with a thickness of two inches (5cm) or more. On the downside, inflating a thick pad may require more than a minute of lung blasting (which, at the elevations you will reach, could give you a nice little case of the dizzies). Lightweight models can be noisy due to crackling material, and punctures are a concern.

Foam Pads – Usually made of dense, closed-cell foams, foam pads can either be rolled up or folded like an accordion. They are light, inexpensive, provide decent insulation, and are practically indestructible from rough surfaces. On the downside, foam pads are usually not very thick and provide limited cushioning comfort. They are not as compressible as air pads and, thus, will require more pack space. However, due to the light weight and durability, these pads are ideal candidates for being strapped to the outside of your pack.

Self-inflating foam pads - Combining the packability of an air pad with the cushioning of a foam pad, while needing only little additional inflation. Thin pads are lightweight and can be compressed into a small sack, but offer limited cushioning. Thicker pads of two inches or more offer more cushioning and insulation, but are heavier.

(i) Whichever option you choose, make sure the pad is long and wide enough to fit your body dimensions. A good test is placing the pad on a hardwood or tile floor and trying it out for a night.

Additional Comfort

Apart from the clothing you wear in your sleeping bag, the only additional sleeping gear you might consider bringing could be some form of pillow, an eye mask, and ear plugs.

An alternative to packing an inflatable pillow is using your sleeping bag's stuff sack as a casing and stuffing it loosely with clothes or buying a sleeping bag with a pillow case pocket sewn inside. I have found the pillow case feature a very nice addition for virtually no extra weight. If you're not wearing your down jacket to sleep, stuffing it inside the pillow case pocket makes for a passable down pillow. If you are extremely sensitive to light, you may consider taking an eye mask if you are traveling during a bright, full moon. If you have trouble sleeping near creeks or streams, you may consider taking ear plugs, but be aware that wearing them will make you less aware of rodents or larger animals in the vicinity.

Lighting in the dark is also important to think about – for camp preparations in the evenings, early or late hiking, reading inside the tent, and for a quick restroom break at night. Headlamps are great because you will have both hands free. In any event, opt for energy-efficient LED light sources, remember to keep your light easily accessible at night, and make sure your batteries are fully charged before you head out.

d. Food & Water

While Section 5b *Food* discussed the type of food and drinks to bring, this section focusses on the gear needed to store, prepare, and eat the food, as well as to treat and store water.

Bear Canisters

Bear canisters are required on the HST. They vary in size, weight, transparent or opaque exterior, locking mechanism, and price. The following are canisters which are approved for use in Sequoia National Park (according to the National Park Service website):

- Garcia model 812 (Backpacker)
- The Bear Keg (Counter Assault)
- Weekender MKII & Expedition MKII (both 1766 or higher; Wild Ideas Bearikade)
- Wise Backpack
- Contender 101 & Champ 202 (Bare Boxer)
- BV 100b, 200, 250, 300, 350, 400, 450, 500 (Bear Vault)
- Little Sami & Big Daddy (Lighter 1)
- No-Fed-Bear (UDAP)

Table 5 below compares four of the approved models between 615-703 cubic inches (10-11.5 liters). With very good preparation and packing, a canister of around 700 cu in. can provide food storage for up to 8-9 days. You will want to get the smallest/lightest canister that will fit all the food you need to carry and has the features that are important to you.

Feature	Lighter 1 Big Daddy	Bear Vault BV 500	Backpacker Garcia 812	Bearikade Custom 703
Total Weight	2lbs 11oz / 1.22kg	2lbs 9oz / 1.16kg	2lbs 12oz / 1.25kg	2lbs / 0.9kg
Interior Volume	650 cu in. / 10.5l	700 cu in. / 11.5l	615 cu in. / 10.1l	703 cu in. / 11.5l
Dimensions [diameter x height]	8.7 x 13 in. / 22.1 x 33cm	8.7 x 12.7 in. / 22.1 x 32.3cm	8.8 x 12 in. / 22.4 x 30.5cm	9 x 11.25 in. / 22.9 x 28.6cm
Housing Material	poly-carbonate	poly-carbonate	ABS polymer	carbon fiber
Transparent	yes	yes	no	no
Tool Free Access	yes	yes	no	no
Price (ca.)	$100	$75	$70	$300

Table 15 – Bear Canister Comparison[17]

---

[17] Information retrieved from respective manufacturer's website

The Big Daddy and BV 500 are both made of transparent polycarbonate, allowing you to see what's inside and where it is – a very convenient feature. Both also have lids that *do not* require a tool/coin to unlock. The BV 500 has a screw-on lid with a click-lock mechanism that requires some well-aimed pressure to open. The Big Daddy uses a couple of small screws. The Garcia 812 and the Bearikade have lids that require a coin or similar tool to open. The Garcia Cache 812 is simple and cost effective. The Bearikade canisters can be custom ordered in many sizes. They are handmade of carbon fiber composite material, making them the lightest but also most expensive canisters on the market.

> ⚠️ Remember, bear spray, pepper spray, and other deterrents are prohibited in several national parks, including Sequoia National Park. Proper use of a bear canister and keeping your campsite food and odor free should be precaution enough. Save the weight of carrying a spray that could harm both you and the wildlife and get you fined.

Stove & Fuel

The preparation of your meals will undoubtedly require a stove, as campfires are generally less convenient and, more importantly, prohibited in certain areas along the HST (see Section 3d *Camping* for details). There are two common stove fuel systems that will be readily available at most outdoor outfitters: gas canisters and liquid fuel. Both are suitable for the HST.

Gas Canisters

Gas canisters are filled with a pressurized gas mix of isobutene and propane. They have a self-sealing valve at the top and thread that you will use for attaching your stove or gas line. Stoves can be screwed directly onto the top of these canisters, using the canister as the base. These stoves are extremely light (<3oz/85g) and pack very small.

Stoves can also be connected remotely. Remote stoves are placed on the ground and connected to the canister via a fuel line. Consequently, the canister can be flipped on its head (referred to as inverted canister).

Inverting the canister allows operation in liquid feed mode, eliminating the need for the gas to vaporize inside the canister. In doing so, the gas can be used at lower (sub-evaporation) temperatures while performance is upheld. Especially in cold conditions, this comes in handy as the output is increased even with only little gas remaining. Compared to stoves that are mounted on top of the fuel canister, remote-fed stoves are also less likely to tip over and easier to shield against wind.

Figure 21 – Canister Stoves: Top and Remote (Inverted) Mounted

The third pressurized gas setup is called an integrated canister system. These systems have an integrated burner and heat exchanger, which are directly attached to the bottom of a pot for optimum heat transfer. These compact units are well-shielded against wind, and their pots are often insulated against heat loss. Integrated canister systems are especially efficient for boiling water. However, it lies in their nature that they cannot be remotely fed and, thus, have limited performance in extremely cold weather.

Generally, all canister systems are easy and fast to use as they don't require priming. They burn cleanly, reach their maximum heat very quickly, and there is no risk of fuel spillage. On the downside, pressurized gas is rather expensive, and gauging how much fuel is left is difficult. Upright mounted canisters (not inverted) bear the risk of tipping over and struggle with the properties of gas, which leads to limited cold-weather operability and reduced performance as canisters empty.

Side Note – Operating pressurized gas canisters in cold weather – understanding the limits:

The lowest operating temperature of a pressurized gas canister is a matter of its gas composition. Good hiking canisters consist of isobutene and propane, while large barbeque canisters often contain n-butane. A canister gas' operating temperature limit is determined by the gas with the highest (warmest) boiling point. Since propane has the lowest boiling point temperature (see Table 16), it will burn off first, especially in an upright canister system.

Boiling Point	° Fahrenheit	° Celsius	Approx. Limit
N-Butane	31	+/- 0	41°F/5°C
Isobutene	12	-11	21°F/-6°C
Propane	-44	-42	-35°F/-37°C

Table 16 – Boiling Points of Stove Canister Gases at Sea Level

A canister with a propane-isobutene mix would reach its limit around 21°F (-6°C) at sea level. As the air pressure drops with increasing altitude, so do the gases' boiling points. So as you ascend, your gas canister will be able to operate at lower temperatures than at sea level. A lapse rate for this effect is to subtract 2°F from the temperature limit for every 1000 ft. in altitude gain (1°C for every 300m).

Typical canister stoves with a propane-isobutene mix are very well suited for the HST. With an operating temperature limit of approximately 1°F (-16°C) at 10,000 ft. (3,000m) elevation, canister stoves will provide reliable heat along the trail. Liquid feed canister stoves can function in even lower temperatures.

! When you are considering temperature in choosing a stove, remember that the fuel temperature, not the ambient temperature outside, is what matters. In very cold conditions, keep your canister inside your tent or even at your feet in the sleeping bag to ensure the gas' temperature is kept as high as possible.

Liquid Fuel

Liquid fuel stoves have a similar setup as remote-fed canister systems. The burner is placed on the ground and connects via fuel line to the bottle fuel tank, which has a pump to pressurize the fuel and a valve to control flow. Most systems require priming, especially in cold conditions. Priming means that a few drops of fuel are placed into a dish underneath the burner and then lit. This heats the attached fuel line and causes the fuel to vaporize at the burner where it can be ignited.

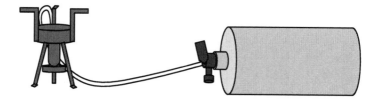

Figure 22 – Liquid Fuel Stove

Liquid fuel systems are dominated by white gas (a.k.a. naphtha). This is a highly refined fuel with little impurities so it burns very clean. There are also multi-fuel stoves that run on white gas, kerosene, diesel, and gasoline. Generally, the greatest advantages of a (petroleum based) liquid fuel stove are the easy international availability of its fuels, low fuel cost, very high heat output, and their ability to operate at low temperatures. White gas, for example, freezes at -22°F (-30°C). Downsides are that some fuels are odorous, smoke, and may blacken pots. The stoves, especially multi-fuel models, are rather expensive. Flames are not as finely adjustable for simmering foods, and overall operation (incl. pumping and priming) needs some practice and bears the risk of flares or burns. Stoves require regular maintenance to avoid clogging, even more so the less purified the fuel is. For these reasons, liquid fuel stoves generally require more experience and effort to use.

With regards to weight, liquid fuel systems are heavier than canisters due to the more complex burner and pump-valve system for the fuel tanks and the heavier fuel. On the upside, liquid fuel tanks are reusable and can be filled as needed, whereas gas canisters can only be bought in a few sizes, making incremental adjustments to fuel quantity difficult.

Fuel Calculation

Once you have decided which type of stove to take, you need to determine how much fuel you will need in order to cook all of your meals. Unless your meals require special preparation, your fuel consumption will be directly proportioned to how much water you will need to boil per day. A good approximation of how much fuel is needed to boil water is 0.012oz fuel per ounce of water (11.5g fuel per liter). If certain meals require simmering after the water has boiled, add 0.035oz (1g) of fuel per minute of cooking time.

Figure 23 shows the equation used to estimate fuel consumption for the duration of your trip. Remember to include any side trips you plan on taking in your calculation. Once you know how much fuel you need, shop for a gas canister or fuel tank that will provide sufficient fuel while minimizing weight.

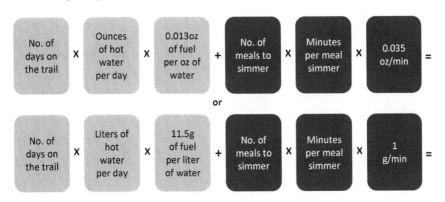

Figure 23 – Estimating Fuel Needs

...na is planning 7 days on the trail. Her estimates for hot water demand per day are as follows:

	8oz	for coffee in the morning
+	8oz	for porridge/oatmeal
+	0oz	for lunch
+	16oz	for a meal in the evening
+	8oz	for one cup of tea
=	40oz	of boiling water per day

Two of her meals each have to be simmered for ten minutes. The rest of her meals are dehydrated/instant meals that don't require simmering. Consequently, her fuel estimate is as follows:

$$(7d \times 40oz \times 0.012oz/oz) + (2d \times 10min \times 0.035oz/min) = 4oz$$

Anna needs approx. 4oz of fuel for seven days. Consequently, Anna could get by with one 4oz (113.5g) canister of fuel (gross weight 13.1oz/370g) for the entire trip.

(i) In order to keep boiling times and wasted fuel low, always use a lid, start on a small flame and increase as water gets warmer, never turning to full throttle. Furthermore, use a screen or heat reflector around your stove and pot to shield the flame from wind.

Lastly, don't forget to bring proper means to ignite a flame. Options include gas lighters, matches, piezo igniters, and spark strikers. Opt for something that is durable, long-lasting, reliable, and water-resistant. It is not recommended to solely rely on only one option. Bring at least one redundant option as a backup in case your first choice gets wet or breaks.

Pots, Pans, and Utensils

Deciding which kind of pot and/or pan to bring depends on how many people you will be cooking for and what you will be cooking. For example, if you are cooking for 1-2 people, one pot of approx. 32oz (0.9l) is sufficient. Most backpacking meals tend be soup or stew-like in consistency and can work with a fairly narrow pot. If you intend to prepare solid meals, you may want to opt for a pot or pan with a wider base. Remember to choose cookware that has an easy-to-clean, non-stick surface.

Whether you are cooking liquid or solid meals, materials such as aluminum or titanium help save pack weight, and using a lid speeds up the cooking time while conserving your fuel. Since pack space will be limited, look for a pot or pan that has a foldable or detachable handle and can be stacked or stored inside other cookware. These features will be pretty standard on any cookware sets that are specifically designed for backpacking. Some are even designed to fit fuel canisters inside to help you reduce pack space even further.

If your cook set is only a single pot, you may also want to consider bringing a small cup/mug (with or without a lid) for hot beverages at camp. This can double as a measuring cup for food preparation and should be extremely lightweight and compact.

While putting together your meals, keep in mind which utensils you will need to prepare and eat them. At a minimum, you will probably want to bring a spoon or "spork" (spoon and fork in one) and a pocket knife. If you are going to be eating directly from your pot or out of the freeze-dried meal pouches, specially designed long-handled spoons will make it easier to get to any food at the very bottom.

(i) You will likely need to measure out quantities of water for preparing some of your meals. If possible, buy a set of pots that have measurement lines marked on them already. Alternatively, you can do some test measuring in your kitchen before you leave, so you know how much water each of your pots holds.

Water Treatment

As discussed earlier in the book, it is advised to treat any water in the High Sierra before consumption. There are six options for doing so: micro-filter pumps, micro-filter gravity and squeeze bags, ultra-violet (UV) sterilization pens, chemical tablets/drops, and boiling. Choosing a water treatment system is just like choosing any other piece of gear – a tradeoff between features, cost, and weight. Below is a brief summary of some of the most relevant differences between the methods:

- Pump filters are fast and work well even in little, murky water, but they are rather heavy and require some maintenance.
- Gravity filters are fast, very easy to use, and the clean tank can double as a hydration pack, but they are expensive and rather heavy.
- Squeeze filters are fast, light, cheap, and filter large amounts of water per cartridge (life span of over 10,000 l/cartridge), but the squeezing is strenuous and the pouch can tear or puncture if squeezed too hard.
- UV lights often come as a pen or integrated in a bottle. They are rather fast and treat viruses, but they rely on batteries to work and somewhat clear water to be effective.
- Chemical options are chlorine dioxide, sodium dichloroisocyanurate, and iodine tablets or droplets. They are very light, cheap, and treat viruses, but work slower than other options and are less effective in murky water. They also usually leave a slight chemical aftertaste. Note, the individual tablet dosage should match your drinking container size. Droplets provide a little more flexibility than tablets in matching the dosage to fit your container size.
- Boiling water should only be a backup option. It is slow, heavy (incl. the fuel needed), and leaves you with hot water to quench your thirst.

Table 17 below summarizes the features and pros/cons of the different water treatment options.

Feature	Boiling	Chemical	UV Light	Squeeze	Gravity	Pump
Speed [l/min]	0.2	0.1-0.25	0.7-1.0	1.5-1.7	1.4-1.8	1.0-1.6
Weight [oz]	0.4/l	2-3	4-6	2-5	8-12	10-15
Treats Viruses	yes	yes	yes	no	no	no
Longevity [l]	n/a	80-100	>10k	>10k	1-2k	1-2k
Ease of Use	easy	very easy	easy	medium	very easy	easy
Durability	long	n/a	fair/long	fair	long	fair/long
Cost	40-50 ct/l	10-15 ct/l	$80-160	$30-50	$80-120	$80-100
Comment	Requires fuel; drinking hot water	Ineffective in murky water; wait time >0.5h; slight chemical taste	Ineffective in murky water; requires batteries / charging	Hard squeezing can lead to pouch tears; hand strength needed	Best if hung, incl. storage bags; great for groups	Pre-filter filters large particles ; requires maintenance

Table 17 – Water Treatment Options

Generally, filters treat protozoa, bacteria, and particles, and allow instant water consumption. Boiling, UV light, and chemical purifiers are effective against protozoa, bacteria, and viruses, but require clear water and additional treatment time. All options, except pumps, are of limited use in very shallow or dirty water, but this is unlikely to be an issue since water is plentiful and usually very clear on the HST.

I prefer to use a squeeze filter in combination with a two-liter filter bladder and a one-liter backup filter bladder. The two-liter filter bladder is the main filter bladder that I use to replenish my fresh water supply. The one-liter bladder is for backup filtering in case my two-liter bladder breaks.

 Keep in mind that if you use a squeeze filter, you should not use the same bladder for both filtered and unfiltered water.

Water Storage

Your water storage options fall into two categories: bottles and hydration packs (also known as water bladders). Whether you choose one over the other or a combination of both will be a matter of personal preference, hiking style, and gear you have available.

Container Options

Practical *water bottle* sizes are 24-48oz (0.7-1.4l). Aluminum, stainless steel, and BPA-free plastic are the most used and suitable materials. Features like narrow or wide openings, sealing valves, and straws are up to personal preference. Insulated bottles are also available but generally heavier and have less capacity. Bottle caps with loops allow attaching to the backpack with a karabiner. Take the lightest weight bottle you can find.

Hydration packs are bags made of puncture-resistant, durable material that are placed inside your backpack and typically include a drinking tube, so you can access the water without stopping to open up your backpack. At the end of the drinking tube is bite valve to control the flow of water. When not in use, the mouthpiece can be clipped onto your backpack strap or clothing for easy access. Having water this readily available is a great first line of defense against dehydration. Typical sizes of reservoirs are 67-100oz (2-3l). Wide openings make for easy filling and cleaning of the packs, and hang loops or specially designed pouches inside the backpack help keep the water reservoir upright. One drawback of using water bladders is that it is difficult to gauge how much water you have left at a given time, since the bladder is hidden in your backpack.

Cleaning and Maintenance

Before hiking: If your hydration pack has a plastic taste, mix a few tablespoons of baking soda, 34oz/1l warm water, and some white vinegar, and let it soak in the reservoir over night; then rinse thoroughly.

After hiking: Clean well and keep reservoir open and as expanded as possible during storage for air circulation, or store the dry pack in the freezer to prevent bacteria from growing.

Water Quantity

In addition to choosing a method for storing your water, you will need to decide how large you want your reservoir to be and how much water to carry in your pack at any given time. The amount you want to carry can vary depending on how much fluid you typically consume on a strenuous hike, the actual hiking conditions (heat, climbing vs. descending), and the distance to your next guaranteed water resupply. Carrying less water and refilling more often (provided, of course, that you know you will be able to refill regularly) helps avoid walking with unnecessary weight that will slow you down and make you more fatigued. In turn, the more frequently you plan to resupply, the more often you will have to stop and unpack your treatment gear, which requires time and effort. Whatever your strategy, keep in mind that the less water you carry, the more important it will be to understand and plan for your water resupply points!

On the HST, I took a three-liter water bladder with hose and carried between one and two liters of water at all times. Every time I stopped to refill, I would drink about a half to a full liter before filling up my water bladder and setting off on the trail again. This helped me minimize the weight I carried on my back while staying well-hydrated. At night, I would filter three liters, one to drink immediately, one to make dinner and breakfast, and one for the trail. By doing all my filtering at once, I reduced the amount of time spent packing/unpacking my water filter system and avoided having to stick my hands into the night-chilled streams early in the morning in order to prepare breakfast.

Emergency Water

If opting for a hydration pack with hose, consider bringing a separate, smaller container as a backup in case the main bladder breaks, starts to leak, or if additional storage capacity is needed for a section of trail with very little water. If I am concerned about the distance between water resupply points, I will carry a small amount of water (½ liter) in a separate container in addition to my main bladder, so I don't have to worry about being totally out of water at some very inconvenient time. Also, in extremely cold temperatures, the water inside the hose portion of your water bladder will freeze, rendering your water bladder virtually useless. Burying a separate water bottle deep in your backpack (for insulation) will help you retain access to drinkable water at below freezing temperatures.

e. Medical & Personal Care

Your first aid kit is one of the few things that you will take on the HST but hopefully never have to use. Nonetheless, a well-equipped first aid kit is vital in an emergency. In addition to bandages and antiseptics, your medical kit should include any personal medications you regularly take or need specifically for this trip. Outdoor outfitters will usually have a basic medical kit that can serve as a good starting point which you can add to or take away from depending on your personal needs. Most importantly, make sure you know how to use all first aid materials you are taking with you, otherwise they won't be of any use on the trail if you get injured. Below are some materials that a good, basic first aid kit will include:

First Aid – Required

- Sunscreen (with high SPF)
- Self-adhesive bandages
- Medical tape (small quantity sufficient for emergency)
- Antibacterial wipe/ointments
- Non-stick sterile pads
- Self-adhering elastic bandage wrap
- Knife (use the pocket knife you already have with you)
- Pain relieving gels/creams (with Camphor, Menthol, Arnica)
- Anti-inflammatories and/or pain relievers (e.g., ibuprofen)
- Blister treatment (bandages, pads, etc.)
- Acetazolamide for altitude sickness
- Survival blanket (silver/insulated)
- Safety pins
- Whistle

First Aid – Specific or Optional

- Any personal medication
- Anti-histamines (to remedy allergic reactions)
- Tweezers (for splinters)
- Insect-sting relief
- Sun relief (e.g., aloe vera)
- Blood thinner (e.g., aspirin)

Personal Care

- Lip balm (with SPF)
- Tooth brush & paste
- Soap (biodegradable)
- Deodorant
- Insect repellent
- Moisturizer

f. Other Essentials

In addition to the basic gear that we covered earlier, the following list of equipment covers some essentials that you should take with you on a long hike through the wilderness.

Gear	Comment
Compass	If you don't already know how to use a compass, I recommend you learn. Knowing how to use a compass is not an invitation to venture off trail. In fact, I highly recommend that you do not venture off trail unless you have significant experience in doing so already.
Maps	Tom Harrison Maps: Mt. Whitney High Country. **This map is a must**. Printed on waterproof, tear-resistant plastic pages, scaled at 1:63,360, the map is durable, small, and covers the entire course of the HST from Crescent Meadow to Whitney Portal as well as some of the surrounding areas that you might decide to add as side trips. Section maps, printed from AllTrails.com: I highly recommend you become a premium member of this site, so you can access the printable National Geographic map database. You will be able to print detailed maps of specific trail sections, showing important trail features (inter-sections, streams, etc.) that a larger map will not. I used these maps *extensively* while I was on the trail to gauge where I was and how much further I had before reaching important milestones. Part of my planning included marking up these section maps with my target camps for each night and distances and elevation gains for each day.
Money and ID	Bring some cash and a credit card for food at the beginning and end of the trail, public transportation or hitch hiking costs, post cards, emergency, etc. Also bring a driver's license or other official form of identification.

Cordage (rope)	A very lightweight piece of cordage (nylon or other synthetic) to hang clothes, replace a strap on backpack, use as shoe lace, or for other emergency purposes.

Table 18 – Other Essential Gear

The following gear is not essential from a survival-on-the-trail, but is worth considering. Whether you decide to take any of these items or not is a matter of personal preference.

Gear	Comment
Camera	A small point-and-shoot camera, a camera phone, an action camera, or a high-quality SLR are potential options. Larger cameras can add significant weight and bulk to your pack and give you a fragile piece of equipment to worry about. Whatever you decide to bring, make sure to bring at least one or more extra battery packs, a solar charger, and a case or other means of protection that also allows easy access while hiking. I took a camera phone, an action camera with two extra battery packs, and a solar charger. The photos and video I have of my trip were well worth the additional weight.
Fishing Gear	A line and some trout lures are sufficient, but you can also go all out and bring a pole. Any fishing requires a license. Unless you are planning a more leisurely trip and are certain that you will fish, I would definitely leave these at home. If you pack anything like I did, cooking fish would be a stretch for the kitchen equipment. For me, the HST was a backpacking trip, not a fishing trip.
GPS Watch	GPS watches can show you distances traveled, speed, pace, elevation, etc. Software allows you to trace your every step back home at the computer and import data into online maps. They are good to have, but not essential for navigating. They have the additional downside of relying on satellite signals for communi-

	cation, which you may not always have in the more remote or canyon areas.
Map App	There are several map apps for common smartphone operating systems; check for recent releases. With your phone's GPS, the app can precisely locate your position on the trail. Some give additional information, e.g., elevation profile. Battery life and reception can be a concern with these devices.
Solar charger	A variety of compact solar chargers with rechargeable batteries and USB power ports are available. Make sure you have enough spare batteries to get you by while your electronic devices charge. You will mostly likely be charging during the day while you are hiking, so make sure you have a way of attaching the solar charger to the outside of your pack. Test the charger out before you hit the trail to make sure it works and is capable of charging all of your devices.
Sunglasses	Sport, tight fit with UV protection, polarized lenses, and a cord to hang them around your neck. The cord will make them faster and easier to take off and put on as you go in and out of shade and help ensure you don't lose your sunglasses.
Toilet Paper	0.5-1 roll max. for the whole trip. Keep a small hand sanitizer in the roll.
Shovel	A small plastic shovel can be used to dig holes in the ground to bury human waste, clean out a fire pit, or dig a small groove to channel water away from your tent. Having said this, I think a shovel is unnecessary weight and generally don't take one. Your foot, a rock, or a stick can be used to accomplish the same thing.
Towel	Quick drying, synthetic fabric, extremely lightweight. I don't take towels when I backpack since my shirt or other clothing will most often suffice for the same purpose.

Table 19 – Optional Gear

7. Personal Experience

This chapter describes my personal preparation, travel arrangements, gear items, and experience on the HST. It is a summary of considerations and efforts that went into my own 5-day journey in June 2014. The below information is intended to provide inspiration, additional guidance, and reference points for shaping your own trip.

a. Plan

Logistics

Since a permit is needed to hike the HST, the first step in my planning process was researching how to get this permit. Once I knew what was involved in getting a permit, I did some research on the trail itself to get a sense of how challenging it would be and whether there were any requirements that I couldn't meet, such as technical/rock climbing ability. In addition, I had to make two important decisions early on in my planning, which would have widespread implications for other aspects of my trip:

- When was I going to hike?
- Was I going to go solo or with a hiking friend?

When was I Going to Hike?

Picking my starting date was a critical step in my planning process. Once I picked the date and got my permit, it put a clock on how much time I had left to prepare, train, purchase and test gear, etc. I opted for mid-June, because I wanted to get on the trail before the summer rush, and I hoped wildflowers and water would be more plentiful earlier in the season.

Solo or with a Friend

As mentioned in Section 4b *Hiking Buddy*, in my experience, having a hiking buddy makes planning for a trip more, not less, complicated. As a result, from the outset, I planned on hiking the HST alone. I did mention the trip to a couple of friends to see whether they were interested in joining, but I did not factor in their attendance to my plans, with the exception that I did reserve a permit for two people (there is no additional cost for doing so), just in case one of them was able to make it. As it turned out, neither could, so I went solo. Had one of my friends been able to join, the only meaningful impacts would have been a slightly lighter pack weight (since we would be sharing some gear) and someone to laugh at me when I tripped over tree roots. In practice, I always prepare for my trips as though I were going alone, taking full responsibility from the very beginning. This has been the best way to ensure that I'll actually do the trip.

Getting the Permit

Due in part to my planning efforts and choices, I encountered no meaningful challenges in preparing for my trip on the HST. The item I paid most attention to was getting a permit. By preparing early and following a specific plan, I was able to secure my permit without trouble. Following the recommendations in Section 4a *Permits & Regulations* should dramatically increase your chances of successfully getting the permit you need.

Transportation to/from the Trailheads

Travel to and from the trailhead was not a huge consideration in my planning. I'm fortunate to live in Los Angeles and have parents with flexible schedules that didn't mind dropping me off and picking me up. Obviously, this was a fairly ideal scenario. Although I thoroughly planned my trip to deliberately avoid any uncertainties, the one area that I left open was how I was going to get from the ending trailhead at Whitney Portal back to Lonepine. As it turned out, I ended up meeting a nice family that allowed me to hitch a ride in their van for a good portion of the way home.

Further Preparation

Because I was going solo and had not undertaken a trip of this length before, I spent a significant amount of energy planning the trip. It was critical that I thoroughly understood the situation I was getting myself into and obtained the necessary tools, experience, and skills to overcome any challenges I might face on the trail.

Once I had decided on a hiking strategy (see Table 20 below), I printed section maps of the entire length of the HST on typical 8½ x 11" printer paper. On each map, I marked my starting and ending points for the day, total mileage, and the approximate elevation gain/loss. On the trail, I used these section maps as a daily guide to track how far I had come, how far I had to go, how challenging the trail was ahead of me, opportunities to refill water, trail junctions, and any important sights along the way. In addition to helping me track my progress, these maps were invaluable in helping me re-adjust my plans when I actually ended up not being able to make it to the campsite I had set for day two.

Campsite	Distance fr. CM (miles)	Elevation (feet)	Day	Distance (miles)
Crescent Meadow (CM)	0.0	6,706		
Mehrten Creek	6.5	7,635		
9 Mile Creek	9.0	7,546		
Buck Creek	10.5	7,200		
Bearpaw Meadow	11.5	7,664		
Lone Pine Creek	13.0	7,395		
Upper Hamilton Lakes	16.5	8,238	1	16.5
Big Arroyo Junction	22.5	9,564		
Moraine Lake	30.5	9,304	2	14.0
Upper Funston Meadow	34.5	6,650		
Kern Hot Spring	37.0	6,916		
Junction Meadow	44.0	8,074		
Tyndall/Lake S. Am. Jct.	45.0	8,822	3	14.5
Wallace Creek	49.0	10,394		
Crabtree Meadow	53.0	10,636		
Guitar Lake	56.5	11,496	4	11.5
Trail Crest (West-Side)	61.5	13,438		
Trail Camp	65.5	12,008		
Outpost Camp	69.0	10,358		
Whitney Portal	72.0	8,373	5	15.5

Table 20 – Personal Hiking Itinerary

Once I had secured my permit, I set about gathering the necessary gear (checking what I had and buying anything else I needed), fine-tuning my plans for each section of the trail, and continuing my conditioning regimen. For anyone who has trained for a marathon or similar significant physical activity, training for your time on the HST will feel quite familiar – you basically want to run the race before you actually run the race. My training essentially amounted to periodic hikes with as much distance and elevation gain as I could find, while carrying a backpack filled with the gear that I would eventually be taking with me. This helped my body get used to carrying my pack load on challenging terrain.

Gear

When it comes to gear, I like to think of myself as a practical hiker. By this I mean that I am fairly weight-conscious and sensitive, but I'm not (yet) the kind of guy that saws the handle off of his plastic tooth brush to save a little extra weight. The gear I purchase tends to be in the high-middle in terms of price, weight, and quality. I have accumulated a good amount of gear over the years and now only buy new gear when I am voluntarily upgrading to a lighter weight version. The only notable additions to my kit were a new ultralight one person tent, a lightweight water filter, a solar charger, and a smaller, lighter pocket knife.

To prevent any avoidable disasters on the trail, I made a point to try all my gear before setting out on the trail. I spent an afternoon setting up and breaking down the new tent a few times. I used the water filter and played around with the pocket knife. I set up the solar charger and experimented charging my action camera and phone to test the effectiveness and time it took to charge. I also checked all the gear that I already had to ensure that it was complete and in working condition. I unpacked and repacked my first aid kit to ensure it had everything I thought was relevant to this hike.

I was generally very happy with my gear, but there are a few things I would do differently next time around or, at least, consider more thoroughly if I were to do the hike again:

Tension-line Tent vs. Internal Pole Structure Tent

In order to reduce weight, I used a tent that utilized one of my hiking poles as the only pole support and relied on tent stakes and tension lines to keep the tent up. While being amazingly lightweight, this tent was not the fastest to set up since pounding in the stakes and adjusting tension lines took a bit of time. I also found it hard to find enough clear room for the tent and the tension lines when I had to camp off-trail at an impromptu location. Lastly, using rocks to pound tent stakes into loose top-soil that hid granite boulders just beneath the surface was a challenge I could have done without at the end of a long day of hiking. The set up and breakdown speed and sheer versatility of an internal pole tent that doesn't rely on tension lines and tent stakes might well be worth the extra weight and room if you can spare it.

Backup Water Bladder vs. Backup Bottle

I took two water bladders, one 3-liter and one 1.5-liter, each with its own hose. My plan was that I could quickly swap to the second bladder and keep hiking without needing to stop and refill water. My plan was flawed in a few ways. First, I could have just as easily disconnected the hose from one bladder and attached it to the other, rather than bring two hoses. Second, I could have used a lightweight water bottle (which I also had with me) as my one backup water carrier, rather than bringing a second water bladder in addition to the water bottle. Third, it never would have made sense to carry two bladders full of water (a combined 4.5 liters) at the same time. Ultimately, the additional weight of an extra water bladder and hose probably made only a marginal difference on the trail, but every bit counts.

One-Piece vs. Two-Piece Cook Set

I took a single pot with me on the HST. While I was able to accomplish everything with this single pot, there were several occasions where it would have been nice to be able to boil water in one while using the other for eating or drinking. Having only one pot meant that I had to wait to have my coffee until after I finished eating my oatmeal. It also meant that I had the pleasure of drinking coffee with little bits of oatmeal floating in it. Since the second piece of my cook set nests with the first, bringing both would add a very marginal amount of weight and require virtually no additional pack space.

Tom Harrison Map

I took the *Tom Harrison Maps: Sequoia and Kings Canyon National Park* map because at the time I was unaware of the *Tom Harrison Maps: Mount Whitney High Country*. While both show you the entire length of the HST, the Mount Whitney map provides a greater level of detail of the area that will be relevant to you on your trip.

My Gear List

Below is a complete list of all of the gear that I took with me on the HST. With the potential changes I mentioned above, I should think that anyone taking this list of gear would be pretty comfortable and not find themselves wanting in any situation they are likely to encounter on the trail. There are certainly better or lighter weight versions of all of these pieces of gear, but I consider this a good upper-middle level set of gear.

Gear	Comments on my Gear
Backpack	65-liter pack with trekking pole storage loops, side water bottle pouches, zippered top and side pouches, internal water bladder pouch, and slit for drinking tube, exterior straps for light gear storage, bottom compartment for sleeping bag, cushioned hip belt with small pouches, and emergency whistle built into chest strap. Weight: 3lbs 9oz.
Tent	Ultralight single person tent that utilizes a hiking pole for center support. It has a solid bottom and a vestibule. Pack size: 15 x 4.5 inches. Weight: 1lb 8oz.
Sleeping bag	3-season down/synthetic mix sleeping bag. Pillow pocket sewn into head area. No padding on bottom since it is designed to be paired with a sleeping pad.

	Temperature rating: 30 °F, 650 fill. Pack size: 8 x 17.5 inches. Weight: 2lbs 11oz.
Sleeping pad	Folding foam pad. Pack size: 20 x 5.5 x 5 inches. Weight: 14oz.
Stove	Mini stove that attaches to the top of a fuel canister. Pack size: 3 x 2 x 2 inches. Weight: 2.6oz.
Fuel	4oz fuel canister. Pack size: 3.5 x 2.5 inches. Weight: 3.9oz.
Fire source	Disposable lighter and waterproof matches.
Pot	Titanium 28 fl. oz. pot with lid. (I did not take a cup with me). Pack size: 5.2 x 4.25 inches. Weight: 5.5oz.
Utensils	Titanium long-handled spoon.
Bear canister	Bear canister with transparent sides and screw on lid. Does not require a tool/coin to open. Pack size: 12.7 x 8.7 inches. Weight: 2lbs 9oz.
Water treatment	Mini squeeze filter. Pack size: 1 x 5 inches. Weight: 2oz.
Hydration packs	1 x 3-liter water reservoir with drinking tube. Pack size: 18 x 8 x 3.5 inches. Weight: 6.5oz. 1 x 1.5-liter reservoir with drinking tube. Pack size: 8.2 x 10.3 inches. Weight: 6.4oz.
Extra foldable reservoir	1 x 2-liter reservoir (for use with squeeze filter) 1 x 1-liter reservoir (for backup use with squeeze filter)
Water bottle	1 x screw lid bottle, glow in the dark. Pack size: 3.62 x 7.87 inches. Weight: 6.2oz.
Pocket knife	Lightweight, folding pocket knife with 3" blade.
First aid/ emergency	Various bandages, medical tape, antibacterial gel, altitude sickness medicine, ibuprofen, survival blanket,

	20 ft. of lightweight nylon cord, 2 extra AAA batteries (for headlamp).
Sunscreen	1oz tube, SPF 50
Camera gear and electronics	Action camera with three rechargeable batteries, smartphone with good camera, charging cables, ear bud headphones.
Maps	Tom Harrison Maps: Sequoia and Kings Canyon, and National Geographic "Topo!" color print outs of each trail section.
Compass	Simple, lightweight plastic compass.
Sunglasses	Polarized sport sunglasses with neck cord.
Bathroom	½ roll toilet paper and waste bag, 1oz toothpaste tube, and toothbrush.
Towel	Small chamois dishcloth.
Headlamp	Lightweight hiking headlamp with red and white light, variable brightness controls, and strobe effect.
Solar charger	Roll up solar charger. Pack size: 4.3 x 1.25 inches. Weight: 3.1oz.
Trekking poles	Collapsible poles. Minimum length: 31 inches. Weight: 19.97oz.
Money & ID	$100 in cash, driver's license.
Clothing	See list in Section 6a *Clothing*
Footwear	Hiking shoes. Weight: 30oz. Lightweight flip flops.

Table 21 – My Gear List with Comments

Here are a few items of gear that I *did not* take, along with comments about why I didn't take them. I would generally consider these optional and know that others might want to take these, but I don't find them necessary.

Gear	Comments
GPS Watch/ Map App	I prefer map and compass to electronic mapping devices for the sheer fact that I don't want to rely on getting a signal in order to be able to navigate in the backcountry. I also prefer to carry the weight of a small plastic compass and a map to a potentially heavier GPS device.
Shovel	You may generally find a shovel useful in order to bury your bodily waste or make some room in a fire pit. In practice, I find that the toe of my shoe, a rock, or a stick can accomplish the same thing in about as much time without much more difficulty. As such, I don't think a shovel is necessary or worth the weight.
Fishing Gear	I planned on hiking at a pretty brisk pace without a lot of downtime to spend on things like fishing. In addition, the one pot I brought would not have been ideal for cooking a fish, and I wasn't sure whether I would be able to start a fire at night.
Soap	I "bathed" at one location on the HST (the Kern Hot Spring) and I did so without soap. I rinsed my pot after meals and wiped it with a small chamois-like cloth but didn't spend the time or effort to wash it out with soap.

Table 22 – Optional Gear List with Comments

Food

Food selection can vary widely by person based on their dietary preferences, how much weight they want to carry, how many calories they want to consume, and other factors. On one end of the spectrum, you might have someone who takes a mountain of energy bars and other snacks and skips hot meals altogether (which also allows them to leave the stove, fuel, and other cooking gear). On the other end, you will have the trail-chef, who wants to have different and interesting options for every meal. I prefer to land somewhere in between, but I tend towards making the meals simple and fast, and I am willing to sacrifice some variety as a result.

I started by assembling a basic group of food for each day that consisted of the following:

Meal	Comments / Type of Meal
Breakfast	Hot breakfast of oatmeal and trail mix along with coffee
Lunch	Energy bars
Snacks	Various dried snacks and energy chews used primarily to augment the energy bars for lunch and add variety
Dinner	Hot dinner (freeze-dried or other) and single-serving juice mixes
Condiments and other items	Powdered milk (used for coffee and one macaroni and cheese dinner)

Table 23 – Personal Food Comments

All of the food for each day (with the exception of the snacks) was grouped together and put in a zip lock bag, labeled with a number for the day that I would eat it, and then packed into my bear canister with the heaviest meals going in last (so they would be the first that I would eat on the trail). I kept all of the snacks together in the top of my pack for easy access during the day and made sure to repack them in the bear canister at night.

Each morning, I would take the bag closest to the top of the canister and eat the entire contents over the course of the day and then repack the bag with wrappers and other trash from the day. The repetitiveness of this routine kept things simple and got me on the trail quickly in the morning and in my sleeping bag quickly at night.

Since my lunches required no cooking, I was able to eat as I hiked or take a brief break just to rest my legs rather than break out all my cooking gear. While the two energy bars were not the most exciting food to have, the addition of a few handfuls of my various snacks over the course of the day made it more tolerable and ultimately served the purpose – giving me energy for hiking.

Meal	My Food	Quantity
Breakfast	Instant oatmeal, trail mix, coffee	2x packets of instant oatmeal for each day plus one handful trail mix 2x instant coffee packets for each day
Snacks	Assorted varieties of snacks	1x small bag of wasabi-flavored dried peas 1x sm. bag of assorted rice crackers 1x sm. bag of chips 3x sm. bag of trail mix 1x sm. bag of raw almonds 3x sm. bag of energy chews 1x sm. bag of dried apricots
Lunch	Energy bars	2x per day
Dinner	Dehydrated entrees or other	3x freeze-dried meals (2 servings each) 1x macaroni and cheese (with added powdered milk) 1x instant mashed potatoes

Table 24 – Personal Food Quantities

b. Go

I awoke to the sounds of a bubbling stream with bird songs floating on the breeze. It was the same alarm I always use. My phone gradually increases the volume until I wake up and turn it off. Despite getting less than a good night's sleep, my eyes popped open easily this morning. I spun my legs off the side of my bed, took a few cautious steps through the darkness, and felt around until my fingers brushed the light switch. Click. I squinted as my eyes adjusted to the light. I glanced over to the dresser where my backpack sat beneath the clean, carefully folded clothes that I would wear for the next several days.

The shuffling noise in the kitchen told me that my parents were already up. It was nice of them to offer to drive me, especially at 3am. They are no strangers to this, I reminded myself. After all, how many times had we left around this same time of night to get up to Rock Creek for our annual camping trip? And besides, Rock Creek was farther. That was five and a half hours. It should only take about four hours to get from Los Angeles to Sequoia National Park.

I spent some time checking and rechecking everything. Was I forgetting anything? Backpack? Check. Sleeping bag? Check. Tent? Check. Food? Check. Permit email? Double-Check. Looks like I have all the import stuff. It was too late to worry about it. We need to get going. Dawn was coming.

I hoisted the pack from my shoulders and lay it sideways in the back of my Dad's Subaru Forester. Man that's heavy. What did I expect? I was going to be carrying everything I needed to survive in the wilderness for several days. I had already ditched all the nice-to-haves in order to reduce weight. No books. No spiffy multi-tool or knife. Just the bare minimum gear and five days of food. My only real indulgence – a GoPro camera and smartphone to document the journey. Sure they were heavy, but how was I going to share all the amazing things I was about to see on this solo trip if I didn't take these? I grabbed my little bag of electronics from the zippered pouch on the top of the pack and climbed into the back seat. My finger pressed one of the buttons. Beep, beep, beep. The GoPro's LCD screen lit up and showed a dimly lit image of my legs. I glanced up as we pulled away from my parents' house. I hope, four hours is enough time to learn how to use this thing.

Day 1: Crescent Meadow to Upper Hamilton Lake (16.5 miles)

At 10am on a sunny June day in 2014, I stepped off the asphalt of the

Crescent Meadow parking lot and onto the dusty soil of the High Sierra Trail. With a quick stop to snap a picture by the sign before heading into the great unknown, I waved goodbye to my parents who had dropped me off at the trailhead and turned my attention to scenery that would hold my attention for the next five days.

Figure 24 – Crescent Meadow

During my first day, the HST took me away from the giant sequoias as I followed the contours of a long, wide valley and made my way towards Bearpaw Meadow. The relatively low elevation and time of day made this section of the trail rather hot, despite the intermittent shade provided by the redwoods and other large trees flanking the trail. A few deer wandered amongst the trunks as I passed – keeping a wary distance, but not even bothering to look my way.

Figure 25 – Trail Overlook

After mistaking one of the many streams that intersected the trail for one that was much further ahead of me (a mistake that I would make repeatedly on day one and a healthy reality check for how slow I was actually traveling), I finally arrived at the ranger station and the Bearpaw High Sierra Camp, a camp-style wilderness "hotel," which is open from June until September and has been hosting guests for over 75 years. I had little success trying to convince the staff to part with a can of beer (they claimed to have none) and politely declined their offer of a bottle of wine (I wasn't about to carry a glass bottle for 72 miles) and so didn't bother stopping. In doing research for this book, I discovered that the amenities and food are only for the guests of the hotel, and they generally won't serve people passing through – just in case you think to ask for something yourself when you pass through. The next beer I would have was destined to be at Whitney Portal and would accompany the first meal that didn't come out of my backpack in several days.

Past Bearpaw Meadow, I crossed Lone Pine Creek and began a steep climb that took me into Valhalla, home of Upper Hamilton Lake, where I swapped the rolling, tree-covered mountains of the lower elevations for the soaring granite peaks of the High Sierra.

Figure 26 – Climbing towards Hamilton Lakes

Exhausted from an overly ambitious distance on my first day, I dropped my pack on the banks of Upper Hamilton Lake and spent fifteen minutes laying on my back in one of the few remaining pools of afternoon sunshine that found its way over the peaks and through the trees.

A few hours earlier, before leaving the Lodgepole Visitors Center, I had a short conversation with the ranger. We'll call him Ranger Bob for fun because I never got his real name:

Ranger Bob: "When you get to Hamilton Lakes, watch out for the deer, because they'll try and eat your clothes."

Me: "Haha! Can you imagine?"

Ranger Bob stares blankly back at me, clearly confused about why I am laughing.

Me (once I realize that Ranger Bob is totally serious about the deer): "Did you say deer are going to eat my clothes?"

Ranger Bob: "Yeah, they like the salt from your sweat, so they'll come up and chew on your clothes if you're not careful."

As I sprinted after the deer, my shirt dangling wildly from the corner of its mouth, yelling expletives that few wild animals have ever been called, I couldn't help but find the situation slightly ironic.

Hamilton Lakes does indeed have sweat-sucking deer, and they really do come straight up to your camp, and they really will, almost defiantly, stare you straight in your face as they begin chewing on your clothes. And if you get close enough and yell at them, they really will take off with your clothes in their mouths. Ever wondered what it's like to wear a shirt that's covered in deer spit? Imagine having about thirty strangers all blow their noses on your back.

On that first night, I stayed awake just long enough to see twilight over the lake and to eat about half of my first trail dinner – a surprisingly tasty freeze-dried Indian dish – but quickly succumbed to a level of tired that could easily have put me to sleep under a midday sun while someone poked me repeatedly with a stick.

Day 2: Upper Hamilton Lake to Moraine Lake (14 miles)

When I awoke, the sun was already touching the highest points of the mountains surrounding the lake, and I set about preparing my first breakfast on the trail. This consisted of the cold remnants of my dinner the night before as well as two packets of oatmeal with a handful of trail mix and two instant coffees with a small amount of powdered milk. The oatmeal and coffee combo was blissfully interesting on this first morning and would become significantly less so by the fourth consecutive day.

Day two took me from the warmer lower elevations to my first major ascent of the trip, Kaweah Gap, across the Great Western Divide and down to Big Arroyo Junction. Realizing that every footstep was taking me further into the wilderness and further away from civilization, an overwhelming sense of adventure set in and, for the first time, I really felt the magnitude of the journey. I smiled and took a deep breath, looking out at the towering rock faces of Valhalla and the deep blue puddle of Upper Hamilton Lake far below.

Figure 27 – Big Arroyo

I continued to wind my way around upper Hamilton Lake and eventually across Hamilton Gorge. During the trail's construction, a steel bridge was erected at Hamilton Gorge to take people across this narrow, steep-sided chasm. An early avalanche made short work of the bridge and sent its mangled remnants into the gorge where they lie to this day. In its place, a tunnel and some additional trail were blasted from the granite walls of the gorge to get hikers from one side to the other. For those who are not thrilled with heights, this will be your first and last real test before you reach Mt. Whitney a few days later.

Figure 28 – Rock Tunnel above Upper Hamilton Lake

Past Hamilton Lakes, I arrived at Precipice Lake – a small body of water just off the trail – which was made famous by photographer Ansel Adam's work *Frozen Lake and Cliffs*. This stunning sight was easily identified by the sheer rock wall that shoots skyward behind the motionless surface of the lake which had fragments of ice still clinging about its edges long after the snow had melted from most of the surrounding mountain tops.

With most of the day's difficult climbing behind me, a few hundred feet more of elevation gain brought me to Kaweah Gap and my passage across the Great Western Divide, a section of the Sierra Nevada that separates the watersheds of the Kaweah, Kern, and Kings rivers. When I crossed through Kaweah Gap, I happened to look off my left and spotted a plaque mounted in the middle of large granite boulder. The plaque is dedicated to Colonel George Stewart – the founder of Sequoia National Park and the namesake of Mt. Stewart, the 12,205 ft. (3,720m) pinnacle just to the north of the pass.

Figure 29 – Trail Leading to Kaweah Gap

I paused for a well-deserved snack as I gazed down the valley stretched out before me, with the lakes of Nine Mile Basin to my left and my final destination for the day, Moraine Lake, presumably concealed somewhere in the distant trees to my right.

After a steady decent from Kaweah Gap, I reached the Big Arroyo Junction, where the HST intersects the waters of the Big Arroyo, and then began the long climb upwards, following the Kaweah Peaks Ridge towards the Chagoopa Plateau. The rushing water of the Big Arroyo gradually faded into silence as I climbed above the trees, following our different paths to the Kern River several miles away.

The 4.6-mile (7.4 km) section of the trail between Big Arroyo Junction and Chagoopa Creek had scarce shade, sandy soil, and limited water, making it one of the least pleasant portions of the HST. It didn't take long to realize that I should take advantage of any of the small streams that I came across (not all of which appeared on my map) since finding the next source of water seemed to be unpredictable.

I arrived on the wooded banks of Moraine Lake as dusk was setting in and spent the remaining light of the day collecting some small branches for a modest campfire. Unlike the previous night at Upper Hamilton Lake, there were no other campers on the banks of Moraine Lake that night. This was both a little disconcerting and satisfying. I hadn't been sure how I was going to feel about being this alone in the wilderness, but I had been sure that I would have nights like these, once I was on the trail. And so, here I was, alone in the woods.

After spotting what I could only assume was bear scat, I decided to return to camp, settle in next to a campfire, and try to stay awake long enough to see some stars. I lasted only slightly longer than I had the night before. This would be my second night of completely failing at star gazing but succeeding at getting the deepest, most satisfying sleep I'd had in recent memory.

Day 3: Moraine Lake to Tyndall/Lake South America Junction (14.5 miles)

Although I had missed the stars the night before, the moon was still surprisingly bright in the dawn sky over Moraine Lake. I made quick work of another couple of packs of instant oatmeal, snapped a few pictures, and headed back to the trail.

Figure 30 – Moraine Lake with Moon

There was nowhere to go but down that morning, and my mind wandered as I descended the 2,000 or so feet from Moraine Lake into the Kern River valley. Periodic "stream" crossings (stream is a bit of an overstatement, but I thought that calling it a "dribble" crossing would just confuse people) and the charred trunks of a recent fire helped make the switchbacks a bit more memorable. The occasional lizard scampering through the dead leaves jolted my attention back to the trail for a brief moment, before my mind once again took to wandering. On more than one occasion, I paused to look up and down the impressive Kern River valley, realizing how relatively few people had ever taken in this view.

Figure 31 – Descending into Kern River Valley

Making a left when I reached the valley floor, I headed north and away from the campsites at Upper Funston Meadow (where I had originally planned on bedding down for night two). Moraine Lake had actually been a backup plan in the event that I didn't make it all the way to Upper Funston Meadow. It turns out that distances and hills are much easier to conquer when you are sitting at a dining table in an air-conditioned home with your map, a red pen, and unchecked self-confidence.

While the vast majority of the HST pushes from west to east, the section along the Kern River runs almost directly south to north. Like a good old fashioned field sobriety test, day three basically amounted to my ability to walk in a straight line. The entire day was spent following the Kern River north as I gradually climbed from 7,000 ft. around Upper Funston Meadow to 8,000 ft. by the time I reached Junction Meadow, where I would leave the Kern River and get back to serious elevation gain.

The 9.3 miles along the Kern River was the hottest, driest portion of the HST. Fortunately, the river was almost always within a couple hundred feet and easily accessible for refilling my water supply. And, although hot, it was hard not to enjoy the looking out across lush ferns beneath the tall pines.

"What a beautiful sea of ferns th... shoot, shoot, shoot, shoot, ...!" It was the only word left in my vocabulary for three full minutes while I stood there, not daring to move. (I didn't actually say "shoot", but the word I did use started with an "s" as well) "It didn't even rattle!? What kind of delinquent rattlesnake lets you get within two feet and doesn't rattle?!" As I watched its long body and unmistakable skin pattern slide away from me, barely visible through a dense underbrush of ferns, my momentary relief at having avoided disaster was quickly crushed by the realization that I was still standing thigh-deep in a sea of ferns so dense that I couldn't see the trail, let alone rattlesnakes with Navy-Seal-quality camouflage, who weren't even going to have the decency to let me know before I stepped on them. "Shoot, shoot, shoot, shoot." One more round for good measure as I blew some time waiting to get up the guts to start walking again. If that rattlesnake ever decides to pick up a copy of Rosetta Stone and give speaking English a shot, there is one word it will never have to practice.

I didn't know it at the time, but once I got close to the bottom of the Kern River Valley and for the entire duration I was hiking alongside the Kern River, I had a very real chance of running into rattlesnakes. Turns out that the elevation along the Kern is plenty low enough to be a viable habitat for rattlesnakes. Awesome, right?! Not too awesome if you are, as I am, pretty petrified of snakes in general. Which is why I was less than thrilled when I ran into not one, but two rattlesnakes in the space of about thirty minutes as I made my way from Upper Funston Meadow towards the Kern Hot Spring. I spent a lot of time worrying about where I was putting my feet on this section of the trail.

The highlight of my day was certainly the Kern Hot Spring. Decades ago, some kind soul(s) constructed a small concrete tub and privacy fence which helped to turn what was a slowly seeping, algae-filled pool of hot water into a little oasis of bliss around the mid-way point of the HST. The hot spring was located just off the trail on the left in a large, treeless, grass-blanketed clearing right next to the Kern River. It would have been really hard to miss it unless I was texting on my phone. Good thing there's no reception.

Figure 32 – Kern Hot Spring

After a bit of examination, I figured out that there was a wooden stopper that I needed to remove in order to let the hot water flow into the tub and another wooden stopper that I was supposed to use to plug the drain hole. (In my mind, this catapulted my status to that of a backwoods Einstein or, at the very least, one of the preeminent plumbing thinkers of our generation. Was plugging and unplugging drains always this much fun? Maybe I missed my calling...) There was also a bucket that I assumed should be used to bring cold water from the Kern so I could mix the two and get that perfect bathwater temperature – although I could scarcely remember what bathwater was supposed to feel like. If you make it to the hot spring, don't forget to drain the tub and re-plug the faucet hole, so that the next passerby doesn't end up having to bathe in your filth.

Still rattled (pun intended) by the rattlesnake encounter, I decided to push on past Junction Meadow to get out of the Kern River Valley to a higher elevation that seemed less likely to have snakes – figuring that the extra effort would be worth the peace of mind as I slept.

This night would be the only one on the HST where I didn't camp in a well-established site. Instead, I made my camp just off the trail junction with Tyndall Creek, where the HST heads west towards Wallace Creek. Had I ventured even five minutes further north, I would have discovered a nice set of campsites in a grove just up ahead. Instead, I learned that setting up a tension-and-stake tent requires a lot more room than I previously thought and is much easier to do in established campsites than in even sparse amounts of vegetation.

I ate my dinner sitting comfortably on a log, glad to feel the crisp cold of the higher elevations once again. With no established campsite and the trail hiding out of view, I realized what it must feel like to truly be in the wilderness; not only miles from civilization, but miles from any trace of civilization. I enjoyed the feeling.

After securing my bear canister under a boulder that would have made Atlas proud, I settled into my now-familiar routine of barely getting the tent zipped up before sleep put an end to the day. The wind rushed through the trees overhead, apparently just as eager as I was to escape the snakes in the valley below.

Day 4: Junction Meadow to Guitar Lake (11.5 miles)

The wind was still blowing when I woke up, so I invited the jacket and beanie to join me for breakfast for the first time. Thanks to the extra push I had made the day before, I realized this would be a pretty short day with only a modest amount of elevation gain before I could pitch my tent on the shores of Guitar Lake at the base of Mt. Whitney.

After spending several minutes moving rocks to reveal my still-there bear canister, I dropped it back in my pack, happily noticing how much lighter it was becoming as I ate my way through the contents. Repetition, although admittedly only three days of it, was making packing and unpacking faster and less laborious. A system was developing. First stuff the sleeping bag, then fold the mat, then this goes here, then that goes there. Then strap the mat to the bag so it can stand upright, which is important so the bear canister can be put in. Then the tent gets squeezed into the gap that's left on the side. Emergency supplies and rain shell go in last for easy access. This was hardly the first or even the fiftieth time that I had packed a backpack before, but I had never felt so totally secure and self-sufficient while staring at a small pile of backpacking gear.

Figure 33 – Timberline Lake

Leaving the Kern River drainage behind, I cut across to follow the Wallace Creek drainage upstream and out of the Kern River Valley. The sparse human sightings I had over the last three days came to an abrupt end as I neared Wallace Creek.

Wallace Creek marks the juncture between the HST, the John Muir Trail, and the Pacific Crest Trail. The three trails overlap briefly between Crabtree Meadow and Wallace Creek, with PCT hikers heading north on their way towards the Canadian border, and JMT and HST hikers heading south to the summit of Mt. Whitney. While certainly not a Los Angeles freeway level of traffic, I did notice a marked uptick in the number of people. I was eager for a bit of human interaction and glad that I decided to spark up a conversation with a few folks as they passed by. Some of them had been on the trail for weeks if not months and gave me a nice glimpse of what my next adventure could be like.

By the time I reached Crabtree Meadow, most of my climbing for the day was behind me and there were only a few hundred more feet of gain over the next few miles until I reached Guitar Lake – the de facto base camp for those summiting Mt. Whitney from the west and the highest elevation yet on my HST journey. I passed by a number of campsites as I descended towards the edge of the lake and found still more as I made my way past. After deciding that I wanted to spend more time relaxing and resting rather than walking back and forth searching for a site, I eventually settled on a site on a small hill at the far side of the lake.

Figure 34 – Campsite at Guitar Lake

Dinner was the best serving of mac and cheese that I have ever had in my life. The food brought memories of my childhood (why didn't I eat this more often?!), and I ate it perched on a boulder overlooking Guitar Lake with the sun setting in the distance. A gentle wind caused the sides of my tent to flutter in the otherwise motionless scene.

Day 5: Guitar Lake to Whitney Portal (15.5 miles)

3,000 feet above me, somewhere out of view, there was a small hut on top of the tallest mountain in the contiguous United States. Today, I was going to see it with my own eyes. But first, time to strap on this headlamp. It was around 1am and I would have been groggier had the cold allowed it. No hot breakfast today. There wasn't time. I was already late. I think. Maybe not. Dang. I should have remembered to look up what time sunrise was. I hurriedly scraped together my gear, shined my headlamp around the site to make sure that nothing was left behind, and set off with two hiking poles in one hand and a half-eaten energy bar in the other.

Ironically, despite all my previous attempts, this was the first time I was awake late enough on the HST to actually see the stars. Seeing the stars in the High Sierra never ceases to impress me. To go from seeing 50 – maybe 100 – stars in the sky over Los Angeles to seeing clusters of thousands so dense I can't hope to pick out a constellation always puts the vastness of the universe into perspective. Although I imagine there would have been about the same number of people around had it been daylight, there was a much greater sense of stillness as I hiked on through the darkness. My footsteps on the crushed granite path seemed extremely loud. For a couple of hours, my experience on the trail was confined to a cone of light that sprung from my forehead and ended about 20 feet in front of me. Beyond that was anyone's guess.

Figure 35 – Switchbacks leading up to Trail Crest

I had a short couple of miles to warm up before the climbing began, and once it began, it wouldn't stop until the summit. The climb to Trail Crest (the pass where you will meet people summiting Whitney from the other side, and where I would eventually descend) is a relentless series of switchbacks that brought me 1,500 vertical feet closer to the summit. At

13,650 ft. (4,160 m), Trail Crest is not only higher than any point I had been on the HST, it is higher than every mountain peak I had seen since I set out from Crescent Meadow. By now, the air had become thin enough that it was my lungs, not my legs, setting my pace on the trail.

Since I knew I would be coming back to this point after summiting, I ditched a bunch of excess weight from my pack (as many do at Trail Crest), making sure to secure everything under rocks so it wouldn't be blown away or carried off by some enterprising rodent. From Trail Crest, I turned left and began hiking the backside of the mountain, looking back down on Guitar Lake which lay an impressive distance below. Although I was stopping much more frequently to catch my breath, the mountain provided plenty of amazing things to look at during these increasingly frequent rest breaks. I took a moment to stop behind the iconic saw tooth spires that lie south of the summit. Gazing between, I could see the valley which would soon lead me back to Lone Pine and the rest of the normal world.

Figure 36 – Backside of Mt. Whitney

Although not yet dawn, it had become light enough that I was able to spot the tin roof of the hut on top of the summit as I neared the peak. The stone-walled hut looks impossibly out of place when you realize that someone (and possibly their hapless pack animals) needed to bring materials up here to build it. Nevertheless, there it stands, as it has since it was erected in

1909 by astronomers from the Smithsonian who were seeking a vantage point with the least atmosphere between themselves and Mars.

With my sleeping bag draped over my head for extra warmth, I sat peering through a small opening in the numerous layers of clothing and bedding, waiting to see the bright dot of the sun appear on the orange, glowing horizon. I made the mistake of pulling a hand out of a glove to activate the camera function on my phone, and spent the next ten minutes wondering if the picture I took was worth the frostbite that was probably going to take the ring finger on my right hand. Fortunately, the other fingers weren't going to let their buddy go so easily and all five piggies made it back home intact.

Seeing sunrise from the summit of Mt. Whitney is one of those moments that will be with me for the rest of my life. While the sheer eastern face made it feel more like the edge of a cliff than the top of a mountain, it only took spinning around to realize that there was nothing in my expansive view higher than where I stood.

Figure 37 – Mt. Whitney Summit at Sunrise

I snapped some pictures of the U.S. Geological Survey Markers on the summit, added a bit more GoPro footage to my memory card, and gave myself a few more minutes of peace to take it all in before beginning the final leg of my journey.

There is almost 6,000 ft. of descent from the 14,505 ft. peak to the 8,600 ft. trailhead of Mt. Whitney's eastern entrance. After doubling back on the portion of the trail between the summit and Trail Crest, I scooped up the gear I had left at the pass and began the descent into the last section of the HST. The remaining 5,000 ft. of elevation loss between Trail Crest and Whitney Portal were a combination of countless switchbacks and a persistently downward sloping trail. 99 switchbacks after I had left Trail Crest (these are surely the "problems" that Jay Z wrote about), I arrived at Trail Camp (12,040 ft.) – the first reliable source of water since leaving Guitar Lake.

Arriving at Whitney Portal, triumphant and exhausted, I stopped in the café for the cheeseburger and beer I had been thinking about for the last three days, as well as some Mt. Whitney souvenirs and other memorabilia that I hope will provide proof to my eventual grandkids that I was, in fact, impressively athletic in my younger years.

(i) If you're interested in knowing more about my trip and really getting a sense of what hiking the HST will be like, I encourage you to take a look at the video from my trip in addition to my personal account included in this book. You will find it on YouTube by entering "Zeb Wallace High Sierra Trail" in the search box. Please note, the video includes a side trip I did after the HST.

Appendices

A. Checklists

These checklists are meant to assist you in your preparations. Depending on the month you are hiking and your personal preferences, you can add or remove certain items from the lists. For those who are unsure about what to pack: if you stick to the lists, you will be in good shape.

Clothing ( ) indicates optional items

	Long sleeve hiking shirt		Gloves
	Hiking pants (convertible)		Sleepwear
	Warm jacket (down or synthetic)	( )	Hiking shorts
	Wind- and waterproof jacket shell with hood	( )	Short sleeve hiking shirt
	Rain pants	( )	Balaclava or multifunctional scarf
	Hiking socks	( )	Sock liners
	Underwear	( )	Glove liners
	Visor or hat (wide-brimmed)	( )	Flip-flops/lightweight sandals
	Hiking shoes or boots		
	Thermal underwear		
	Thermal long sleeve top		
	Beanie/warm cap		

Personal Items (optional)

	Notepad and pen		Mirror
	E-reader		Tripod
	Headphones		Book

Gear ( ) indicates optional items

	Backpack	( )	Camera
	Shelter (tent/bivy/tarp)	( )	Extra batteries & memory card
	Sleeping bag	( )	Trekking poles
	Sleeping pad	( )	Mug (with lid)
	Camping stove	( )	Shovel
	Fuel	( )	Towel
	Lighter/matches	( )	GPS watch/other watch
	Cooking pot	( )	Solar charger
	Eating/cooking utensils	( )	Map app
	Bear canister	( )	Fishing gear
	Food	( )	Sleeping gear (ear plugs, inflatable pillow, etc.)
	Water treatment system	( )	Spare water container (collapsible)
	Hydration pack or water bottles	( )	Medication
	Head lamp	( )	Deodorant
	Pocket knife		Insect repellent
	First aid kit and personal care items	( )	Moisturizer
	Tooth brush and paste	( )	Soap (biodegradable)
	Toilet paper	( )	Silver survival blanket
	Sunglasses		
	Sunscreen		
	Lip balm (with SPF)		
	Print-outs for all travel arrangements		
	Map		
	Compass		
	Photo ID		
	Money		

Food List per Day per Person (3 alternatives per meal)

Breakfast	
	2 slices of bread and peanut butter
	2 packets instant oatmeal + trail mix
	Freeze-dried scrambled eggs

Lunch	
	Jerky + crackers
	Energy bars
	Dried hummus with 2 tortillas

Snacks	
	Nuts and seeds
	Dried fruit
	Protein/granola bars

Dinner	
	Freeze dried instant meal
	1½ cups quinoa, dried veggies + broth
	2 cups pasta, dried tomatoes + herbs

Other Food Items / Condiments

	Sugar
	Coffee (and creamer)
	Tea (no caffeine for evenings)
	Hot chocolate
	Olive oil
	Salt & pepper

	Spices & herbs
	Hot/soy sauce
	Vitamins & minerals
	Parmesan cheese flakes
	Powdered milk

B. Food Suggestions

Breakfast

- Instant oatmeal (purchase with or add flavors and sugar), porridge, semolina, and polenta with dried fruits
- Self-mixed grains/cereals - with sesame, chia, flax, sunflower, pumpkin and other seeds, raisins and other dried fruit and berries, nuts, coconut flakes; rolled oats, shredded wheat, multi grains, etc., mixed with dry milk, powdered soy, coconut, or almond milk, and possibly protein powder
- Pumpernickel (dark rye bread), tortilla, pita, or other dense, long-lasting breads
- Almond and peanut butter, tahini (sesame paste), chocolate spread, jelly and honey
- Freeze-dried breakfasts (e.g., scrambled eggs, hash browns)
- Tea bags, tea pouches (such as ginger granulate), coffee, hot chocolate

Lunch

- Smoked/dried sausage (e.g., traditional salami), beef and other jerkies
- Tuna and salmon in pouches, dried salted fish and shrimp
- Powdered hummus (add water and olive oil)
- Crackers (wheat, whole grain, corn), breads and tortillas
- Aged cheeses which do not need refrigeration
- Energy or nutrition bars

Snacks

- Almonds, pistachios, other nuts and seeds (no shells, with/without flavors, smoked)
- Dried fruits (mango, apricot, banana, date, fig, apple, etc.) and berries, fruit leather

- Power bars and gels; protein, granola, and cereal bars; other candy and snack bars
- Sundried tomatoes, veggie chips, rice crackers, dried peas, dried seaweed snacks
- Chocolate, gummy bears, caramel bonbons (limit these "empty calories")

Dinner

- Freeze-dried/dehydrated instant meals in pouches – just add boiling water (try different varieties, flavors, and brands before you go)
- Pasta with sundried tomatoes, tomato paste, and/or pesto, olive oil and spices, parmesan cheese
- Quinoa, millet, and couscous with herbs and spices with packet tuna (add dried carrots, onion, peas)
- Soup base or stock cubes, add noodles or rice and flakes of mushroom, parsley, tomato, etc.
- Ramen noodles and other instant dishes (e.g., macaroni & cheese, dried mashed potatoes)
- Burritos with rice, packet chicken, beans, cheese, dried bell pepper
- Mixed lentils, beans, and chickpeas with seasoning (keep in mind the cooking times)
- Condiments: salt, pepper, spices, mustard, ketchup, hot sauce, soy sauce, olive oil, chili flakes, parmesan (I don't recommend taking these separately, every meal should be pre-seasoned and self-contained)
- Herbal tea, instant hot chocolate

C. Elevation & Campsites

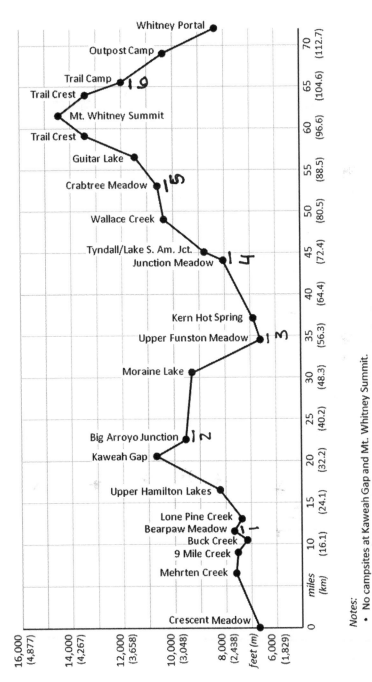

Campsite	Distance from CM		Approx. Elevation		Bear Box avail.	Water avail.	Campfire OK
	miles	km	feet	meters			
Crescent Meadow (CM)	0.0	0.0	6,706	2,044	Yes	No	No
Mehrten Creek	6.5	10.5	7,635	2,327	Yes	Yes	Yes
9 Mile Creek	9.0	14.5	7,546	2,300	Yes	Yes	Yes
Buck Creek	10.5	16.9	7,200	2,195	Yes	Yes	Yes
Bearpaw Meadow	11.5	18.5	7,664	2,336	Yes	Yes	Yes
Lone Pine Creek	13.0	20.9	7,395	2,254	No	Yes	Yes
Upper Hamilton Lakes	16.5	26.6	8,238	2,511	Yes	Yes	No
Big Arroyo Junction	22.5	36.2	9,564	2,915	Yes	Yes	Yes
Moraine Lake	30.5	49.1	9,304	2,836	Yes	Yes	Yes
Upper Funston Meadow	34.5	55.5	6,650	2,027	Yes	Yes	Yes
Kern Hot Spring	37.0	59.6	6,916	2,108	Yes	Yes	Yes
Junction Meadow	44.0	70.8	8,074	2,461	Yes	Yes	Yes
Tyndall/Lake South America Jct.	45.0	72.4	8,822	2,689	Yes	Yes	Yes
Wallace Creek	49.0	78.9	10,394	3,168	Yes	Yes	Yes
Crabtree Meadow	53.0	85.3	10,636	3,242	Yes	Yes	Yes
Guitar Lake	56.5	91.0	11,496	3,504	No	Yes	No
Trail Crest (west side)	61.5	99.0	13,438	4,096	No	No	No
Trail Camp	65.5	105.5	12,008	3,660	No	Yes	No
Outpost Camp	69.0	111.1	10,358	3,157	No	Yes	No
Whitney Portal	72.0	115.9	8,373	2,552	Yes	Yes	In camp

Note: Distances are rounded to the nearest half mile.

D. Trail Crossings

Trail Crossing	Comment
Crescent Meadow Loop Trail	This trail splits off shortly after you set out from the Crescent Meadow trailhead.
Wolverton/ Giant Forest	This trail will head uphill from the HST about 1/5 of the way between Crescent Meadow and Hamilton Lakes.
Alta Trail/ Panther Gap	You will encounter this trail approximately 1/3 of the way between Crescent Meadow and Hamilton Lakes.
Little Bearpaw Meadow	The junction for Little Bearpaw Meadow takes off from around Bearpaw Meadow.
Elizabeth Pass Trail	Shortly after Bearpaw Meadow, you will encounter the trail to Elizabeth Pass and/or Lone Pine Meadow.
Big Arroyo Trail	You will pass a short connector trail that will take you on the Big Arroyo Trail right around Big Arroyo Junction.
Moraine Lake Trail	As you descend towards the Chagoopa Plateau, keep an eye out for the Moraine Lake Trail on your right. **You will want to take this trail if you are going to camp at Moraine Lake.** Moraine Lake is a great place to camp if it fits into your schedule.
Upper Funston Meadow	When you reach the Kern River, take the left fork of the trail junction to stay on the HST. The right will take you on the Lower Kern Trail towards Upper Funston Meadow. **If you are going to camp at Upper Funston Meadow, you should make a right instead of a left.**
Colby Pass Trail	Around Junction Meadow, keep an eye out for the Colby Pass Trail taking off from your left.

Shepherd Pass Trail	Once you have climbed out the Kern River Valley, keep an eye out for the intersection that will let you head to the west and follow the HST to Wallace Creek, the JMT and/or the PST. You do not want to go towards Tyndall Creek or follow the Shepherd Pass or Lake South America Trails. **This particular trail junction is one of the easiest to miss.**
HST/JMT Intersection	Around Wallace Creek you will intersect with the John Muir Trail (JMT). Make sure you take the JMT heading towards Mt. Whitney.
JMT/PCT Intersection	Around Crabtree Meadow, the JMT will intersect the Pacific Crest Trail (PCT). Make sure you stay on the JMT and take the trail heading towards Mt. Whitney.
Trail Crest	When you reach Trail Crest on the backside of Mt. Whitney, take the trail to reach the summit. You will come back to this intersection to descend the mountain.
Mountaineers Route	Just before you reach Whitney Portal, you will pass the junction of the Mountaineer's Route, an alternative way to summit Mt. Whitney.

E. Side Trips

California is home to a huge number of world-class destinations. Your trip on the HST can easily be extended to include recreational activities at some of the nearby National Parks or any number of attractions to be found in Los Angeles or San Francisco. Below are just a few of the places you may want to consider.

General Sherman Tree

The General Sherman Tree is a giant sequoia in Sequoia National Park. It is the largest known living single stem tree by volume anywhere on Earth. It is approximately 275 feet (83.8m) tall and 25 feet (7.7m) in diameter. This tree is located just off the highway that you will need to take between the Lodgepole Visitor Center (where you will pick up your permit for the HST) and the trailhead at Crescent Meadow, making it an easy stop along the way before you embark on the HST.

Death Valley National Park

Death Valley National Park is the lowest, hottest, and driest place in the United States. On July 10, 1913, a weather station in the park recorded 134 °F (56.7 °C) – the hottest temperature ever recorded anywhere in the world. The sheer severity of the Park's features and scenery make it an attraction worth seeing. The park lies to the east of Lone Pine – the first town you will come to after finishing the HST.

More info: *http://www.nps.gov/deva/index.htm*

Yosemite National Park

About 3.7 million people visit Yosemite National Park each year, drawn to its stunning scenery and famous features, like Half Dome and El Capitan. The park is to the north of the HST and due east of San Francisco, giving you the opportunity to visit it either before or after your trip on the HST.

More info: *http://www.nps.gov/yose/index.htm*

Devil's Postpile National Monument

This National Monument takes its name from a very interesting columnar basalt rock formation created thousands of years ago by volcanic lava flow. Devil's Postpile is a few-hour drive to the north of Lonepine, the first town you will come to after finishing the HST.

More info: *http://www.nps.gov/depo/index.htm*

Manzanar National Historical Site

Just off highway 395 on your way back to Los Angeles from Whitney Portal, you will pass by a small stretch of land called Manzanar. Manzanar was used as an internment camp for Japanese Americans during World War II, because the government was afraid they might conspire against the U.S. to aid Japan.

More info: *http://www.nps.gov/manz/index.htm*

F. Naismuth's Rule

Naismuth's Rule says that a hiker of good physical fitness should allow 1 hour for every 3 miles (4.8km) forward, plus 1 hour for every 2,000 feet (610m) of ascent. Mr. Naismuth must have been one hell of a hiker, because that pace is extremely fast considering that you will be hiking with a full pack up and down mountains. Because of this, many consider Naismuth's Rule to be more like the minimum time you need. As a result, we will be modifying it here to make it more useful and realistic.

The table below is based on Naismuth's rule but has been modified to account for different levels of fitness as well as carrying a full pack at high altitude. The modifications include reducing the miles per hour (to account for the pack weight, altitude, and fitness level), reducing the elevation gained per hour (to account for fitness level), and adding breaks (to account for this not being a forced march through the mountains).

		Fitness Level		
		Average	Good	Very Good
Total Miles you Want to Travel		11.50	11.50	11.50
Miles per Hour*	/	1.25	1.50	2.00
Total Hours Needed for Distance		9.20	7.70	5.75
Total Elevation Gain During Hike (feet)		1,393	1,393	1,393
Elevation Gain per Hour** (feet)	/	1,000	1,500	2,000
Total Hours Needed for Elevation Gain		1.40	1.00	0.70
Hours Needed for Distance		9.20	7.70	5.75
Hours Needed for Elevation Gain	+	1.40	1.00	0.70
Hours of Breaks During the Hike***	+	1.00	1.00	1.00
Total Hours Needed for Hike		11.60	9.70	7.45
Total Miles you Want to Travel		11.50	11.50	11.50
Total Hours Needed for Hike	/	11.60	9.70	7.45
Trail Hiking Speed** (Miles per Hour)**		**1.00**	**1.20**	**1.50**

* Miles per Hour is the miles you can hike in one hour on flat trail at high elevation while carrying a full pack.

** Elevation Gain Per Hour is an estimate of how much time it will take you to gain elevation during your hike.

*** Hours of Breaks During the Hike include stops for lunch, relaxing, and resting.

**** Trail Hiking Speed is an estimate of the miles you can hike in one hour, including elevation gain and breaks.

As an example, we're going to use the modified version of Naismuth's Rule to estimate how long it might take a person of "good" fitness to hike the first 11.5 miles of the HST (the distance from Crescent Meadow to Bearpaw Meadow, where they plan to camp).

Assuming they did some test hikes and figured out that they hike around 1.5 miles per hour while carrying a full pack, it should take about 7.7 hours to cover the 11.5-mile distance (11.5 miles / 1.5 mph = 7.7 hours).

In addition, they know that there is about 1,400 feet of elevation gain between Crescent Meadow and Bearpaw Meadow. Using our modified Naismuth's rule, they see that they should add about one additional hour to account for this elevation gain.

Lastly, they would like to stop for a relaxing lunch along the way and also plan on a taking a few photos, so they add an extra hour to their schedule.

When they add it all up, it looks like it will take about 9.7 hours to reach their campsite at Bearpaw Meadow, which equates to a pace of about 1.2 miles per hour. They will use this information to determine how early they need to hit the trail, how much time they will have at Bearpaw Meadow before it gets dark, and the pace that they need to maintain during the hike.

For this table to be useful, you must have a reasonable understanding of your own hiking pace. Take a full pack on a few training hikes in the mountains to get a feel for how fast you'll hike on the HST. Keep in mind that hiking with a group will make your pace slower, since people will need to stop at different times for rest, photos, and restroom breaks, and the group will move at the pace of the slowest person.

G. Links & References

National Park Service Sequoia & Kings Canyon

The National Park Service website has a wealth of information and resources for Sequoia & Kings Canyon National Parks (SEKI). Using the link below you can access the permit application, trail use restrictions, descriptions of the trail, trail conditions, and other helpful information:

-- *http://www.nps.gov/seki/planyourvisit/wilderness.htm*

Specific information on flora and fauna:

-- *http://www.nps.gov/seki/learn/nature/index.htm*

Specific information on the HST:

-- *http://www.nps.gov/seki/planyourvisit/high-sierra-trail.htm*

Specific information on the General Sherman Tree:

-- *http://www.nps.gov/seki/learn/nature/sherman.htm*

Specific information on hiking/camping restrictions:

-- *http://www.nps.gov/seki/planyourvisit/upload/2015-Minimum-Impact-Restrictions-FINAL-2.pdf*

Specific information on wilderness permits and availability:

-- *http://www.nps.gov/seki/planyourvisit/wilderness_permits.htm*

Specific information on bear canisters:

-- *http://www.nps.gov/seki/planyourvisit/bear_bc.htm*

Sequoia Parks Foundation

Additional information about the formation and history of Sequoia National Park.

-- *http://www.sequoiaparksfoundation.org/2010/historic-people-and-places-george-w-stewart/*

Camping and Lodging Options

Camping in Sequoia:

-- *http://www.nps.gov/seki/planyourvisit/campgrounds.htm*

Hotel and other lodging in Sequoia:

-- *http://www.visitsequoia.com/reservations.aspx*

Camping at Whitney Portal:

-- *http://www.recreation.gov* (search for 'Whitney Portal')

Sequoia High Sierra Camp:

-- *http://www.sequoiahighsierracamp.com/*

Bearpaw High Sierra Camp:

-- *http://www.visitsequoia.com/bearpaw.aspx*

Wild Backpacker

Detailed information for the Mt. Whitney section of the HST.

-- *http://www.wildbackpacker.com/backpacking-trails/mount-whitney-trail/*

Recreational Equipment, Inc. (REI)

Wide-ranging outdoor advice & products:

-- *http://www.rei.com/learn/expert-advice.html*

Weeden, N. (1996) *A Sierra Nevada Flora,* Wilderness Press

A detailed guide to the flora of the Sierra Nevada. While compact, it may not be light enough to take on the HST with you but could give you a good idea of what are likely to see along the trail.

Tweed, W. (1982) *A Guide to and History of the Western Third of the High Sierra Trail Crescent Meadow to Kaweah Gap, Sequoia National Park,* Sequoia National History Association, Inc. Three Rivers, California.

This book provides only a very rudimentary description of the fascinating plants, animals, and other natural wonders you will see on the HST. If you're interested in learning more, the following publications will provide significantly more detailed information about these features of the Sierra Nevada.

Storer, T. I. (2004) *Sierra Nevada Natural History (California Natural History Guides),* University of California Press

A great all-around overview of the plants, animals and topography of the Sierra Nevada. While compact, it may not be light enough to take on the HST with you but could give you a good idea of what are likely to see along the trail.

Richins Jr., P. (2008) *Mt. Whitney: The Complete Trailhead to Summit Guide,* Mountaineers Books

A comprehensive guide to Mt. Whitney. Useful information regarding best places to camp on multi-day backpacking trips, interesting exploratory side trips, and route variations that either reduce the length of a given route, avoid difficult terrain, or add additional "must-see" areas.

And, of course, visit

www.PlanAndGoHiking.com

for more information, pictures, and posts.

We look forward to and appreciate your feedback!

H. Contact Information

Dow Villa Motel (for additional long-term parking if Whitney Portal is full)
310 S Main St
Lone Pine, CA 93545
Phone: +1 (760) 876-5521

Giant Forest Museum (Sequoia National Park)
Generals Hwy
Three Rivers, CA 93271
Phone: +1 (559) 565-4480

Lodgepole Visitor Center (for permit pickup)
63100 Lodgepole Rd
Sequoia National Park, CA 93262
Phone: +1 (559) 565-4436

Mt. Whitney Ranger Station
Highway 395 & CA-136
Lone Pine, CA 93545
Phone: +1 (760) 876-6200

Sequoia and Kings Canyon National Parks
47050 Generals Highway
Three Rivers, CA 93271
Phone: +1 (559) 565-3341

I. List of Abbreviations

CA	California
ETD	Estimate of Trail Days
g	gram
HST	High Sierra Trail
Jct.	Junction
JMT	John Muir Trail
k	kilo (= thousand)
kg	kilograms
km	kilometers
l	liter
m	meters
NPS	National Park Service
PCT	Pacific Crest Trail
SEKI	Sequoia & Kings Canyon National Parks
YDS	Yosemite Decimal System

About the Author

The son of a botanist and a biologist/author, Zeb was brought up with an appreciation for nature, an enthusiasm for exploring the world outside, and a well-honed ability to sit on the smoke-side of campfires for hours at a time. He was camping and riding his parent's shoulders on hikes through the Sierra Nevada before he could walk.

Zeb and his family have camped at Rock Creek (near Bishop, California) every year since he was a child – a tradition that they continue to this day. These trips made him a more capable and confident hiker and developed his interest in exploring longer and more challenging trails. Zeb enjoys the stillness and focus that can be found on a long, difficult hike alone through the wilderness. He considers the following to be some of his most memorable treks:

- Mt. Kilimanjaro (Tanzania, Africa)
- High Sierra Trail (California, United States)
- Cactus to Clouds Trail (California, United States)
- Zion Narrows (Utah, United States)
- Mt. Whitney (California, United States)
- Bright Angel Trail, Grand Canyon (Arizona, United States)

Zeb lives in Los Angeles, California, a few miles from where he grew up. When he's not backpacking or working, he enjoys going on local hikes, running with friends, and planning for his next adventure.

Contact info: *zebwallace@gmail.com*

Special Thanks

I'd like to acknowledge a few people who were instrumental to my journey on the HST. It was their contributions and influence in my life that led me to attempt, successfully complete, and ultimately write a book about the High Sierra Trail.

To my mom and dad, Marianne and Gary Wallace, who, through years of repeated exposure to camping, hiking, and the out-of-doors, have instilled in me a deep appreciation for the Sierra Nevada and for the wilderness in general. An additional note of thanks must be given to my mom, who is an author herself and a constant source of inspiration and encouragement in all my creative pursuits.

To my brother, Ben, for making every camping trip fun way before I was camping on my own. Who knew sticks, rocks, and imagination could be a source of so much enjoyment.

To the Sierra Club's Wilderness Travel Course (shout out to the West Los Angeles Group 1 class of 2014, "The Down Booties") for giving me the additional skills and experience I needed to be able to undertake this trip with confidence. I can't say enough about this organization and the quality, enthusiasm, and generosity of their staff.

To the LAFunners, a small but fantastic group of friends who run and eat brunch with equal enthusiasm. Our marathons and weekend runs on the beach made the 72 miles less intimidating.

To the Schenk family for providing additional details for certain elevations and distances on the trail.

To "Lone Pine Kurt" for providing some great insight into the transportation options to and from the trailheads.

Disclaimer

The information provided in this book is accurate to the best of author's and publisher's knowledge. However, there is no aspiration, guarantee, or claim to the correctness, completeness, and validity of any information given. Readers should be aware that internet addresses, phone numbers, mailing addresses, as well as prices, services, etc. were believed to be accurate at time of publication, but are subject to change without notice.

References are provided for informational purposes only. Neither author nor the publisher have control over the content of websites, books, or other third party sources listed in this book and, consequently, do not accept responsibility for any content referred to herein. The mention of companies, organizations, or authorities in this book does not imply endorsement by author(s) or publisher, and vice versa.

This book is not a medical guidebook. The information and advice provided herein are merely intended as reference and explicitly not as a substitute for professional medical advice. Consult a physician to discuss whether or not your health and fitness level are appropriate for the physical activities described in this book; especially, if you are aware of any pre-existing conditions or issues.